"People caring for people. Compassion and lovingkindness in difficult circumstances. This is the medicine we need the most, and it is administered on every page of *Angels in the ER,* a chronicle of mankind at its best."

—RICHARD THOMAS
Film, television, and stage actor
"John-Boy" on *The Waltons* and host of *It's a Miracle*

"*Angels in the ER* is hard to put down. You are *right there* with Dr. Lesslie in every circumstance, and each situation shows the spiritual dimension of life and death in a way most of us will never experience on our own. I can only compare the demand for moment-to-moment decision-making with my time on the basketball court. I enjoyed every story."

—BOBBY JONES,
Cofounder 2XSALT, four-time NBA All-Star, and member of the 1983 World Champion Philadelphia 76ers

"In an age when patients are viewed as Social Security numbers, Dr. Lesslie recovers the fading image of a caring doctor for whom the patient is center stage…If I ever land in an emergency room, I hope Dr. Lesslie is there waiting for me."

—RANDALL RUBLE,
President, Erskine College and Seminary

"We meet an amazing cast of characters who come through the doors of a South Carolina hospital emergency room…But Robert Lesslie is also there, a faithful, empathetic physician with a heart for compassion and a keen eye for the presence of God in the midst of human need."

—THOMAS LONG,
Bandy Professor of Preaching,
Candler School of Theology, Emory University

Angels in the ER

Robert D. Lesslie, MD

HARVEST HOUSE PUBLISHERS

EUGENE, OREGON

Cover by Left Coast Design, Portland, Oregon

Cover photo © Ryan McVay / Digital Vision / Getty Images

Back-cover author photo © Penny Young

This book is not intended to take the place of sound professional medical advice. Neither the author nor the publisher assumes any liability for possible adverse consequences as a result of the information contained herein.

All the incidents described in this book are true. Where individuals may be identifiable, they have granted the author and the publisher the right to use their names, stories, and/or facts of their lives in all manners, including composite or altered representations. In all other cases, names, circumstances, descriptions, and details have been changed to render individuals unidentifiable.

ANGELS IN THE ER
Copyright © 2008 by Robert D. Lesslie, MD
Published by Harvest House Publishers
Eugene, Oregon 97402
www.harvesthousepublishers.com

Library of Congress Cataloging-in-Publication Data
Lesslie, Robert D, 1951-
Angels in the ER / Robert D. Lesslie.
    p. cm.
Includes bibliographical references.
ISBN-13: 978-0-7369-2315-6 (pbk.)
ISBN-10: 0-7369-2315-2
1. Hospitals—Emergency services—Popular works. 2. Emergency medical personnel—Popular works. I. Title.
RA975.5.E5L47 2008
362.18—dc22

                                                                    2007052796

Printed in the United States of America

            09 10 11 12 13 14 15 16 / VP-SK / 11 10 9 8 7 6 5

To Barbara—
The angel in my life

Contents

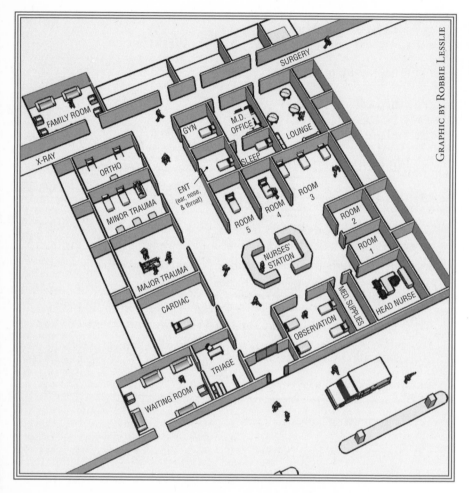

Layout of the Rock Hill ER

Angels in Our Midst

Twenty-five years in the ER have taught me a lot of things. I know without a doubt that life is fragile. I have come to understand that humility may be the greatest virtue. And I am convinced we need to take the time to say the things we deeply feel to the people we deeply care about.

I have also come to believe that there are angels in our midst. They may take the form of a friend, a nurse, or a complete stranger. And on occasion, they remain unseen, a subtle yet real presence that instructs, comforts, and protects us.

The ER is a difficult and challenging place to be, both for patients and for those of us who care for them. Yet the same pressures and stresses that make this place so challenging also provide an opportunity to experience some of life's greatest wonders and mysteries. It is with a sincere appreciation of these mysteries and a profound sense of privilege that I offer some of my thoughts and experiences in these pages.

—Robert Lesslie, MD
March 2008

1

The **Nature** of the **Beast**

*Even though I walk through the valley of the shadow
of death, I will fear no evil, for you are with me.*

—PSALM 23:4

Everyone in the department turned to the ambulance entrance. We had all heard the screaming and shouting, especially the piercing wail of a young woman. Suddenly the automatic doors burst open, and a crowd of fifteen or twenty people, all teenagers or maybe a little older, spilled into the ER. In their midst they carried a young man. His arms and legs dangled wildly, and his head rolled from side to side. His T-shirt was soaked with blood.

"Somebody, help!" The cry came from someone near the front of the pack. "Jimmie's been shot!"

We all moved in the direction of the door. Jeff Ryan, the charge nurse this night, was the first to reach the wounded man. "Follow me," he instructed the people carrying Jimmie. "And don't drop him."

He led the group toward the trauma room, and called over his shoulder to the unit secretary, "Get Security!"

At the doorway, Jeff turned and took the bleeding boy into his arms and then carried him to the middle of the room. As he was carefully placing the young man on the stretcher, a few members of the crowd tentatively stepped into the trauma room.

"Nope." One word from Jeff stopped them in their tracks. "You guys will need to wait outside."

Few people questioned Jeff Ryan's authority. He was in his early thirties, stood six feet tall, and weighed about two-twenty-five. He had been in the ER when I first came to Rock Hill, and I soon came to appreciate the fact he was one of the finest nurses I would ever work with. He looked like a big teddy bear, but something in his eyes let you know that beneath that gentle exterior lurked a rugged strength and potentially explosive temper. I've seen it explode a few times…and woe to the person in its path. We referred to Jeff as our "enforcer."

Within a few minutes, Jimmie was completely undressed, lying on his back. He had an IV line in each arm, each rapidly infusing normal saline. A catheter had been inserted into his bladder and oxygen was being administered through nasal prongs held in place by an elastic strap encircling his head.

I examined his abdomen for the second time. One bullet hole, just above his belly button. This was an obvious entrance wound, and there was no exit. He had been awake and talking since we placed him on the stretcher. His vital signs had been fair at the outset, with only a mildly depressed blood pressure. This had quickly improved with the IV fluids, and now things appeared to be stabilized. The lab techs had come down and they were now cross-matching blood for transfusion. We would give it as soon as it was available. The on-call surgeon, Sam Wright, had been notified. Fortunately he was still in the hospital—in the operating room finishing up a case.

A few minutes later he was on the phone.

"Sam, this is Robert," I spoke into the receiver. "I've got a nineteen-year-old male here in the ER with a single gunshot wound to the abdomen. He's alert and his vital signs are stable, but there's no exit wound. The X-ray looks like the bullet's lodged somewhere near his right kidney. And it looks like something small, maybe a .22." I was making a guess about the caliber but in reality, it didn't make much of a difference.

"Get him ready for the OR," Sam replied through the speaker-phone. "Looks like we'll have to open him up and see what's going on. I'm closing up the appendectomy you gave me earlier, so I'll just meet him here in the operating room."

"Okay, we'll do that. He should have gotten about a unit of blood before you see him."

"Fine." Then he was gone.

Jeff was making some notes on our patient's clipboard.

"Dr. Wright ready to see him in the OR?" he asked me.

"Yeah, as soon as everything's in order," I answered.

He picked up the board, stepped over to the side of the stretcher, and checked to be sure both IV lines were flowing. Then he headed for the door.

"I'll get some help and we'll get him going," he told me as the door was closing.

I looked down at Jimmie and asked, "Are you sure there's nobody we need to call? Family? Relatives?"

He had already been asked this several times and each time had told us that no one needed to be bothered. The "friends" who had brought him to the ER were of no help either. Once Jimmie had been deposited in our trauma room they had disappeared. Maybe they had heard Jeff request Security, or maybe they knew that a police squad would soon be on its way. Whatever the reason, they were gone.

We were alone in the room, and I was waiting for the transport team to come.

"Doc, I'm not gonna make it," he stated matter-of-factly.

This blunt pronouncement surprised me. I glanced down at him, checking his color, and then over at the cardiac monitor to be sure I wasn't missing something. He seemed stable enough.

"Jimmie, you're going to be fine. I know this is no fun for you, but it's a straightforward wound, and Dr. Wright will get you fixed up. You may have nicked some intestine or something like that, but he'll patch things up, and you'll be going home in a few days." I didn't have to try to sound confident, because I was. This would be a basic surgical procedure. Unfortunately, we saw too many cases just like this. He would be fine. He was young and healthy.

Now peaceful and calm, he continued to stare straight up at the ceiling. His arms rested at his sides, and a sheet was drawn up to his waist. He had a lot of tubes connected to him, but he was stable and looked good.

"No, man," he said, quietly resigned and still staring at the ceiling. "I'm not gonna make it out of that operating room." His tone and words bothered me. He needed to be encouraged.

"Jimmie—"

Before I could finish, the door opened and the two men of the transport team came into the room. They made the necessary preparations and began pushing the stretcher toward the door. I stood out of the way.

Jimmie was halfway through the door when he twisted his head around and looked directly at me.

"Not gonna make it, Doc."

"Everything's going to be fine, Jimmie," I told him once more, and then he was gone.

Of course I was right. And I would be able to tell him so in a few hours. I looked at the clock on the wall. 12:30 a.m.

At 1:00 a.m., a nineteen-year-old girl hobbled into the department and was led to room 2 by our triage nurse. She had stepped in a hole (which happened to be just outside one of our town's drinking establishments) and sprained her right ankle. It was pretty swollen, and we would need an X-ray to make sure it wasn't broken.

We had no sooner sent her down the hall in a wheelchair to X-ray than the ambulance doors swung open. EMS brought a twenty-five-year-old woman directly to the cardiac room. She had a long-standing history of kidney disease and extremely high blood pressure. Tonight she had apparently suffered a stroke. She was breathing, but was not responding to pain or verbal stimulation. We would need a CT scan of her head, and quickly.

Within a few minutes, her stretcher was heading down the hall toward Radiology.

I stood at the nurses' station, writing on the charts of these two patients. A busy evening was turning into a busy night.

Suddenly, an unfamiliar voice bellowed behind me, almost in my ear.

"Where's my baby? Where she be?"

Startled, I turned around and found myself nose-to-nose with a middle-aged woman. She was dressed in a blue-and-white-striped bathrobe, barely held closed with two large safety pins. A black silk nightgown could be seen extending below the bottom edge of the robe, almost sweeping the floor. And on her feet she wore bright-red bedroom slippers, fashioned after some fuzzy, unidentifiable animal.

But my eyes were drawn to her head. Her hair was in curlers, huge pink ones, held in place by something I couldn't quite make out. I looked a little closer, and I recognized it—it was a large pair of women's panties.

"Where is Naomi?" she asked no one in particular. "Her friend-girl said she was over here!"

She began to look around the department, searching frantically for her daughter. She stepped toward one of the exam rooms and was about to pull the curtain aside when I was able to stop her.

"Ma'am, I'm Dr. Lesslie. Come with me, and we'll help you find your daughter."

She stopped and looked at me, about to speak. Then she turned her head slightly to one side and looked over my shoulder. Her eyes widened hugely.

"My baby!" she screamed, pointing down the hallway. "What have you done to my baby?"

She swept me aside with one large arm and ran down the hall, bumping me into the counter.

"My baby! What have you done to her?" she screamed.

Our young stroke victim was returning from CT. She lay flat on the stretcher, still unresponsive, and was being rolled up the hall to her room.

"Look at her! You killed her!" She was screaming even louder now. She barreled through the radiology techs, brushing one aside as she grabbed the girl's face in her hands.

"She dead! You killed her!"

There was an instant of silence. Her eyes rolled back in her head, and her face turned to heaven.

And then a piercing wail, "Do Jesus! Help me, Lawd!"

Jeff was moving toward the woman. He would try to calm her and then lead her to a private room. This type of outburst was not unusual in the department, and though disconcerting, we had all grown accustomed to it. But this was all new to our other patients, and a few inquisitive heads peered from behind curtains, trying to get a glimpse of the scene. They didn't want to get too close, though. This woman was on fire.

"Who did this? Who killed my baby?"

Jeff walked to her side and quietly said, "Ma'am, she's not dead. We're taking good care of her." He patted her gently on her shoulder.

She would have none of this and jerked away from his hand.

"I want to know who did this!" Her voice was becoming menacing. Then she looked directly at me and took a step in my direction. She pointed a threatening finger at me and said, "I'm gonna sue you! I'm gonna own this hospital! And you're gonna be sorry." There followed some choice descriptives of my heritage, and then she turned again to the young woman, patting her on the forehead. Once more she lovingly took the girl's head in her hands.

"Baby, what they done to you? What they done to you? I'm gonna—"

She stopped in mid-sentence and froze where she stood. Then her head tilted from side to side as she studied the face of the girl lying before her. A puzzled look began to spread across her face, and her eyes began to widen in surprise. Suddenly, she was distracted by a movement further up the hallway and looked up. It was our ankle-injury patient. She was returning to the ER in a wheelchair, her X-rays in her lap.

Our distraught mother stood straight up, dropping the young woman's head back on the stretcher.

"*There's* my baby!" She ran up the hallway, smiling in relief, her arms extended before her. The safety pins that had been barely holding her bathrobe together had finally given up and the robe flew open, flapping wildly at her sides as she ran. When she got to the wheelchair, she knelt and embraced her daughter. She hugged her tightly, rocking her back and forth.

"You all right, honey baby? You okay?"

There was nothing to say or do. We just stood there.

It was 4:30 a.m., and I was beginning to flag a little. One more cup of coffee and I might live to see the sunrise.

I was turning to walk towards the lounge when I saw Sam Wright coming up the hallway. He still wore his surgical cap and scrubs. They were soaked with perspiration, and I noticed splashes of blood from his knees down to his shoe covers.

He collapsed into one of the chairs behind the nurses' station, pulled off his scrub cap, and tossed it into a nearby trashcan.

"Man, that was tough," he said, shaking his head.

I walked over and sat down beside him. He was talking about Jimmie. "What did you find, Sam?" I asked.

"We got him to the OR and onto the table. As soon as we put him to sleep, his pressure started to fall. Not much at first, but then it really crashed. When I opened him up, there was blood everywhere. I tried to cross-clamp the aorta to even begin to see what was going on. The bleeding was coming from a place I couldn't get to, and I never got complete control of it."

He paused and looked up at me, shaking his head.

Then he continued. "That bullet nicked the side of the aorta and then lodged just below the kidney. It didn't hit anything else. Amazing. The nick must have immediately clotted off, and he didn't do much bleeding. Not until he got to the OR. The clot came off, and everthing broke loose. Eight units of blood. As fast as we got the blood into him, it was on the floor. We tried everything. We worked…" he paused, looking at his wristwatch. "We worked on him for three-and-a-half hours."

He stopped, and his shoulders slumped forward. He stared unseeing at the floor.

"This is a tough one, Robert. I don't know what else I could have done."

We sat there, silent. Jeff came up the hall with two cups of black coffee and set the steaming Styrofoam cups on the counter. Neither of us moved.

"And you were right." Sam spoke again. "It was a small-caliber bullet—.22, I think."

The ER and Rock Hill and the rest of the world moved on around us. And I thought of the last words Jimmie had spoken to me.

The ER. It all happens here. This is an amazing place to observe and study the human condition. We see and experience every feeling and emotion, and do so in an intense and highly charged environment. Gone are the trappings of proper decorum and behavior. Gone are the concerns about what others may be thinking about us. Where else would you see a fifty-year-old banker walking down the hallway in a hospital gown, uncaring that his derriere was exposed to a bunch of strangers?

But we are all undressed in the ER, all of us. Our strengths and weaknesses are openly and sometimes uncomfortably exposed. This is true for patients and physicians alike. As caregivers, whether nurse or doctor, orderly or secretary, we quickly learn the limits of our willingness and ability to empathize, to sacrifice, and to step outside of ourselves. It is possible to remain aloof, distant, and shielded…but it comes with a price.

Ultimately, the ER is a place where the faith of each one of us will be tested. Our beliefs will be tempered and refined, or exposed and discarded as worthless. Here we can learn who we are and on what ground we stand. And sometimes, it is a place where our faith can be found.

These pages tell the stories of people who have traveled into this dark valley. Through their experiences and struggles, we can search our own hearts for answers to finding grace and peace in the darkness.

2

The **Least** of **These**

*I was hungry and you gave me something to eat, I was thirsty and
you gave me something to drink, I was a stranger and you invited
me in, I needed clothes and you clothed me, I was sick and you
looked after me, I was in prison and you came to visit me.*

—MATTHEW 25:35-36

The ER is a lot of things to a lot of people, but one of its most
important functions is to serve as a safety net for those who have
nowhere else to go. These are the people with no money, no insurance, no family, no friends. The ER offers the best and last chance
they have for medical care. Sometimes it's the only place they have
for care of any kind.

It may be difficult to imagine someone would consider the ER
a place for comfort and companionship, but a good example of this
occurs every Christmas. Most people would want to be at home, or
with family and friends, you'd think, and a trip to the ER would be
an unpleasant necessity only because of dire illness or injury. But
that's not the case for a large and largely invisible part of our society.
Mid to late morning will see a steadily growing stream of people who
should be elsewhere.

They have no one else to spend Christmas Day with than whatever
staff happens to have the misfortune of being on duty in the department. They have no other place to find a holiday meal, bland and
unexciting though it may be. And when you take that closer look, and
you try to imagine what life must be like for this man or woman, and

especially what word you should speak or action you should take, it can get pretty uncomfortable.

◆◆◆◆◆

It was two in the afternoon on a cold and clear Tuesday in February.

"General, this is Medic 1, over."

I recognized Denton's voice and picked up the ambulance telephone. Denton Roberts was one of the lead paramedics for the hospital's EMS. He was in his mid-thirties, bright, aggressive, and his assessments in the field could always be trusted. He had attended Clemson for a couple of years and given some thought to applying to medical school. Once he started working as a paramedic, though, he knew he had found his niche.

"Medic 1, this is Dr. Lesslie, go ahead," I responded.

The receiver crackled briefly. "Dr. L, we're bringing in a 65-year-old man with abdominal pain." There was a momentary pause. "It's Slim."

That was all he needed to say. I looked around the department to see which bed was available. "Bring him to room 2, Denton. What's your ETA?"

"About five," he said. "Room 2 it is."

I placed the phone back in its cradle.

Slim Brantley was one of our "regulars." He had been a regular since I began working at Rock Hill General. Depending on the time of year, we might see him once or twice a week. When the weather was good, he might go a month or so before calling an ambulance and coming to visit. We were in the midst of a cold snap, and this would be his third visit in the past nine days.

Lori walked up to the nurses' station with a clipboard in her hand.

"We've got a friend coming in," I told her.

"Slim?" she guessed, placing the board in its rack.

"Yep," I answered. "Again."

"Well, it's been two days, so I guess it's about time. Abdominal pain?" she queried, knowing the answer.

"Bingo."

Lori Davidson had been working in the ER for seven or eight years. She was the mother of three young children, a boy and two girls. She had a quiet, unassuming demeanor, and yet she displayed a confidence and compassion that immediately put our patients at ease. I was always glad when she was on duty.

"I'll get Slim's room ready," she told me.

It requires a significant effort to reach the exalted status of "ER regular." Not just anyone achieves this lofty appellation. At any given time, we probably have only ten or twelve people in that circle. Just the fact that you come to the ER on a frequent basis does not necessarily make you a regular. We have drug seekers who do just that, but we don't consider them regulars. That's a whole different set of problems. Our regulars come to the ER over and over again with generally the same complaint. It might be abdominal pain, as in Slim's case, or alcohol-related issues, or back pain, or seizures. It can be any of a number of things. But each of our regulars has developed their own unique handle.

For years, one of our favorite and most persistent regulars was a woman named Sarah May. She was in her sixties and lived with her older sister. At some point, she had become convinced that a root doctor practicing in Rock Hill (I'm not sure if he was board-certified in that specialty) had put a snake in her. I think it was a black snake. But she was absolutely positive a snake was crawling around in her belly. She would writhe on the stretcher, rub her abdomen, and plead with us to get the snake out of her. What do you do with that? Invariably, she came to the ER by ambulance, usually a little after midnight. EMS would call in with "We have a woman here, in no apparent distress. We're at 100 Pine Street." That was all we needed: her address.

"It's Sarah May again," would be the universal response. And in about fifteen minutes, she would be rolling into the ER.

Over the years, things changed with Sarah. On several occasions, I had her committed to a psychiatric hospital in Columbia for an evaluation. After a week or two, she would end up back home. She didn't like this experience, and didn't like being committed to a mental hospital. Apparently they had as much luck getting that snake out of her as we did. Eventually she developed the practice of calling the ER before she called EMS.

"Is that Dr. Lesslie on duty tonight?" she would ask our secretary. When the answer was in the affirmative, there would be a pause, a faint sigh, and then "Oh, well..." followed by a click. And no visit that night. But there were plenty of other visits for her, and her ticket to the ER was always that snake.

Slim Brantley, for whatever reason, had chosen abdominal pain as his handle. Or maybe it had chosen him. Though he had been worked up on numerous occasions, no pathology had ever turned up. He did have some real disease, though. Too much alcohol and three packs of cigarettes a day had taken their toll. He had very little lung reserve and had become very susceptible to pneumonia. And his heart had been giving him problems lately, as shown by recurrent episodes of a rapid heartbeat and dizziness. Those things were real. But his abdominal pain was not. It was his free pass to the ER, and it got him in the door and into a bed. And in short order, it usually got him a warm meal. After an hour or two, his pain would be gone, he would feel better, and he'd be ready to go home.

I have often wondered where someone like Slim lives. One evening, Denton Roberts and I were sitting behind the nurses' station. For whatever reason, the conversation turned to Slim, and Denton told me about the time he had picked him up under a bridge. It had been midsummer, and Slim had constructed a lean-to of cardboard boxes. Apparently, based on the litter surrounding this impromptu abode, canned beans and Ripple wine had been his sustenance for several days. On another occasion, he had been picked up in someone's garage, where he was sleeping on a ratty cot between two broken-down lawn mowers. The owner of the house had provided this shelter in exchange for the few odd jobs Slim was still able to perform.

I had no idea what he did when it was really cold. Apparently he had some friends who would provide a place to stay until he made them mad or started a fire in the basement, and then they'd kick him out.

We tried everything with Slim: social services, charity organizations, and on many occasions, detox. We even had him committed to a mental hospital once. But nothing worked. It was never very long before he ended up back in the ER.

And here he was on his way in again tonight. We were busy, but it shouldn't take too long to evaluate Slim and get him squared away. Now this is where I had to be careful. When medical students or first-year residents rotate through the ER, I have to constantly remind them that even our "regulars" get sick, and you have to be vigilant in your assessment of them, as with every patient. Maybe more so. I have to remind myself of that as well. The temptation, of course, is to blow them off as "just the usual" and move on to the people who *really* need your help. Sometimes that approach can be disastrous. It had proved disastrous for another of our ER regulars, Faye Givens.

Faye was a middle-aged woman who had visited our ER on a frequent basis for years. Her complaint was always "nerves," and by the end of her visit, she would invariably ask for "a sleeping pill." Sometimes a simple Tylenol tablet would suffice, and she would happily go on her way. At other times, she would become adamant about receiving a shot for her condition, becoming quite loud and disruptive. To my knowledge, she had never been diagnosed in our ER with any serious condition.

One evening she came in by ambulance, complaining of her usual "nerves." This time, however, she added the complaint of a severe headache, pointing to her forehead. Dr. Canty, one of my younger partners, was on duty, and like the rest of us, he knew Faye very well. His cursory exam did not elicit any bothersome findings, and he was prepared to try giving her a Tylenol and send her home.

He instructed Lori, on duty that particular evening, to do just that. She went to Faye's room but immediately came back to the nurses' station, her medicine cup still containing the small white tablet.

"I'm just not sure about Faye tonight," she told him. "Something's just not right about her. Maybe you'd better take another look at her."

Dr. Canty stopped what he was doing and looked at her. A part of him responded to Lori's concern, trusting her proven judgment. A small cloud passed over his previously clear decision, causing him to second-guess himself momentarily. But this quickly passed, and he blew off this interruption. He had seen Faye on many occasions and it was always the same—no emergency, no serious medical problem. It was always just a disposition dilemma—how to get her out of the department with as little trouble as possible.

Yet he respected Lori. Partly to placate her and partly to dispel any remains of that bothersome cloud, he walked over to where Faye was sitting on the edge of her stretcher. Her head was hanging, lolling slightly from side to side. Even this posture was part of her usual behavior.

"Faye, how is that headache?" he asked her.

"Doc, it's killin' me. Like somethin' is stickin' in the middle of my head. Can't you give me somethin' for it?" she pleaded.

He reached out and took her head in his hands, once more making sure her neck was completely supple. It was. And then he looked again at her eyes. Amazing! They were crossed, and she was able to hold them that way! That took a real effort. Her look was comical, and he tried desperately to suppress a chuckle.

An Academy Award–winning performance, he thought to himself.

"I'll be right back," he told her, walking out of the room and over to Lori.

"She's fine," he said, a tone of finality in his voice. "Go ahead and give her the Tylenol and let her go."

Reluctantly, Lori did as instructed, and Faye was soon on her way home.

Two days later, she returned to the ER, dead. Her autopsy revealed she had a large tumor pressing on the ocular structures in the front of her brain. That was what had caused her eyes to be crossed, and was what killed her.

I was behind the closed curtain of room 5 when I heard the clicks and wheezes as the automatic ambulance doors opened. Then I heard Denton as he confirmed his destination with Lori. "Room 2?" he asked her.

"Yes," she answered. "That's fine."

"Ooooooooo!"

It was a moan I would recognize anywhere. Slim.

"Oooooooo! My belly!"

I finished giving instructions to the patient in room 5, pulled the curtain aside, and stepped out. Turning back to the middle-aged man on the stretcher, I said, "Go ahead and get dressed. A nurse will be right with you." I pulled the curtain closed behind me.

Denton had deposited Slim on the bed in room 2, and Lori was taking his temperature. My eyes caught Slim's and he furtively looked away.

"BP's 110 over 70," Denton informed me. "And his pulse is about 90, but a little irregular. He looks okay to me," he added, holding the EMS clipboard in his hand while I signed the bottom of the transport sheet.

"Okay, Denton. Thanks."

He pushed the stretcher out of the cubicle and moved toward the nurses' station while I stepped into Slim's room. Lori had replaced the blood-pressure cuff in its holder on the wall and was attaching two electrodes to his chest, connecting him to the cardiac monitor.

"114 over 72," she told me, turning on the monitor and then making a note on a paper towel that had been hastily placed on the countertop. "No fever. 98.4."

"Oooooooo! Doc, do somethin'! It's killin' me!"

The monitor came to life, and its *beep-beep-beep* drew my eyes to the screen mounted on the wall over his head.

I thought immediately of Rita Flowers.

Rita was a recently graduated RN, rotating through the ER as part of her hospital orientation. She was a bright young woman, but the jury was still out as to whether she had the judgment to be a good critical-care nurse. At this point in her career, she was of course quite green, and very naïve.

On one particular day, she had the good fortune to take care of Slim. He had come in by ambulance with his usual complaint of abdominal pain. She was quite concerned by his writhing, vociferous demonstrations, and she hurriedly checked his vital signs and connected him to his monitor. Her obvious concern was not lost upon him.

She had hastily stepped across to the nurses' station and grabbed the nearest available physician.

"Doctor, you need to come and see this man!" she pleaded. "Now!"

The ER doctor had looked over her shoulder and readily identified her patient.

Turning back to the chart on the counter, he said, "It's okay, Rita. I'll be there in a few minutes."

She stood there, not knowing what to do. She looked around for help, but everyone seemed busy. Racing back to his cubicle, she glanced at the cardiac monitor. It was now nice and regular. That was good.

Slim continued to moan, his eyes closed, his hands clutching his belly. Slowly one eyelid crept up, and he waited for his opportunity.

Rita turned to the countertop by the side of the stretcher and began making some notes. Slim slowly reached up to his chest and grasped one of the monitor electrodes attached there. He jiggled it forcefully and cried out in agony.

"Ooooooo!" he yelled, rolling from side to side.

Rita looked at him, and then instinctively at the monitor on the wall. All kinds of wavy lines were crossing the screen! She had never seen anything like it before. What was she supposed to do? Call a code? And then suddenly there was a nice, quiet, regular rhythm. Slim's moaning stopped. Rita breathed a sigh of relief.

"Please get me somethin' for this pain," he pleaded.

Rita glanced at the nurses' station, and then back at Slim.

"I'll see what I can do, Mr. Brantley."

She turned again to her charting. Slim waited a moment, and then again jiggled the electrode.

"Ooooooo!" Louder this time.

Rita looked at the monitor and there were those same strange, undulating waves. His heart was going in and out of some peculiar, chaotic, and obviously dangerous rhythm. Something terrible was going to happen if she didn't do something. And then he was quiet, and the monitor resumed its steady *beep-beep-beep*.

That was enough.

"I'll be right back," she told him, stepping toward the entrance of the cubicle, on her way to get some help.

She was met by Virginia Granger, head nurse of the department.

Virginia, our most seasoned veteran, held up her hand, stopping Rita in her tracks. She nodded at Rita and then indicated that she needed to follow her back to Slim's bedside. She had been observing the whole affair.

Virginia indeed presented an imposing figure. She had turned sixty a few weeks earlier, and to her chagrin she had unsuccessfully kept her age a secret from the ER staff. Ramrod straight and always wearing a blindingly white and overstarched blouse and skirt, there was no mistaking her military background. She had worked in various army hospitals for more than twenty years and had brought that bearing and organizational experience to our ER. And she had brought the same pointed, black-trimmed nurse's cap she had worn constantly since graduating from nursing school.

Virginia stood over Slim, hands on hips, lips pursed, and brow furrowed. She was a menacing sight.

"Slim Brantley," she said, drawing out his name for effect.

His eyes slowly opened, and his chin sank to his chest. A schoolboy caught in the act of thumping the head of the girl sitting in front of him.

She waited a moment, then took his hand away from the electrode on his chest and placed it by his side.

"Slim, I don't want you to ever do that again," she admonished him. "Ever."

Slim, still the little boy, said, "I won't, I promise."

Virginia nodded solemnly, winked at Rita, and then stepped out of the room.

Rita just stood there, staring down at Slim for a moment, perplexed and confused. When she finally realized what had been happening here, she turned to follow Virginia back to the nurses' station.

"Ma'am," a small voice behind her whispered. "Could I get somethin' to eat?"

I had taken care of Slim for the past fifteen years, and amazingly he never seemed to change. He was six-foot-four, maybe six-five. You couldn't really tell. Even when he was "well," he slumped over, his long arms dangling by his side. And he was really skinny. He had probably never weighed more than 170 pounds on any occasion I had seen him. His face was wrinkled, craggy, and his eyes had the smoky appearance of too much booze over too many years. His teeth, those few left in his head, were yellowish brown and in sad repair. His hands were quite remarkable. His fingers were extremely long, as were his ridged and filthy fingernails. The index and middle fingers of his right hand were stained a deep and dirty yellow, attesting to a steadfast relationship with his Marlboros.

Today Slim seemed especially unkempt. His clothes were layered for the cold weather. He had on two pairs of trousers, the outermost a stained and torn green plaid. His black boots were well worn and, surprisingly, they matched. More surprisingly, the soles were intact. He had no socks. He wore two light-blue sweaters, the outer one at least two sizes smaller than the inner. Under this was what appeared to be an umpire's jersey.

"Doc, can you give me somethin' for this pain? It's worse than ever! Ooooooo!"

I examined Slim, asking him where he had been staying, when the pain had begun, and whether there were any associated symptoms. The usual things I needed to know. All the while, I perfunctorily confirmed that his exam was normal, or at least as normal as it could be for Slim.

Convinced nothing serious was going on, I picked up the clipboard for room 2 and began writing. "Slim," I said. "Your belly checks out okay. Doesn't seem to be anything bad going on. Do you think if you had something to eat, you would feel better?" Somehow, I knew the answer to this question.

Slim began to rub the hollow that was his stomach. "Well, Doc, ya know, that would probably do me a lot of good. The pain seems to have eased a little. What do you think they're servin' in the kitchen?" He looked hopeful and a lot more comfortable.

"I don't know, Slim, but I'll try to find out."

Walking over to the nurses' station, I pulled his curtain closed behind me.

"Amy, would you call down to the cafeteria and see if they could send up a tray for Slim?" I asked her.

"Already on its way," she replied. "A double."

Like me, Amy had helped take care of Slim for a lot of years. She was thirty-two years old and one of the best unit secretaries who had ever sat behind the nurses' station in the ER. And that was saying a lot. It took a lot of savvy, patience, and gumption to handle the almost constant barrage of telephone calls and frantic orders being thrown at her. In addition to possessing all of those important traits, she was also our resident NASCAR enthusiast. In quieter moments she would sometimes remind us of the time she shook the hand of Junior Johnson.

Thirty minutes later Slim was eating, quiet and content. The department had gotten busier. A cardiac arrest was on its way in, and we had two patients with carbon-monoxide poisoning who had been fortunate enough to make it to the ER to be treated. They should recover without any problems.

As I came out of room 3, I walked past Slim's curtain. I was stopped in my tracks by an offensive odor. I looked around and then glanced at the nurses' station. Amy was staring at me. She was shaking her head, pinching her nose with one hand and pointing accusingly at room 2 with the other.

"Not again!" I said to her, exasperated.

She simply nodded in response.

One of Slim's major problems over the past few years was the development of an untimely loss of bowel control. Untimely in that it usually occurred in our department, right after he had eaten. To his credit, he was always apologetic.

My opportunity to reflect upon this unwanted circumstance was cut short by the bursting open of the ambulance entrance doors. Two paramedics hurried a stretcher toward the cardiac room. It was our heart attack.

The patient was a ninety-two-year-old man with extensive cancer and advanced Alzheimer's disease. There was nothing we could or should do for this elderly gentleman. I instructed the paramedic to stop chest compressions, and we studied the monitor. Flat line. We watched for a few minutes but nothing changed. He was gone. He had no family members, and no one would be coming over from the nursing home.

Thanking the EMS crew, I started writing up his record and walked back to the nurses' station.

As I passed room 2, I happened to glance over and was able to see through the partially parted curtain. I stopped and watched.

Lori was in the room with Slim. Gloved, she was cleaning him up from his gastrointestinal mishap. And she was smiling at him.

"Ma'am, I'm awful sorry about this," he said to her, his eyes lowered, looking away. It's hard for a man to maintain his dignity when he's sitting in the middle of a public place with his pants down.

"Slim, it's alright," Lori said, still smiling. "Accidents happen. And I'm just glad you're feeling better."

She continued to clean him. The odor was still terribly strong.

Then she was finished, and she peeled off her gloves and tossed them in the contaminated waste container. She washed her hands in the sink and was stepping toward the entrance of the room when she paused, stopping by the head of his bed. She put her hand on his shoulder, patting it gently.

"Slim," she said softly. "You need to take better care of yourself. You need to stop your drinking."

"I know, Ma'am, I know. It's just hard," he responded. "But I'll try."

"Good, Slim. That's all we want you to do. Just try."

Lori had been down this road many times with Slim. And yet she was still offering her support, again demonstrating that somebody cared about him.

She turned from the stretcher and took her hand away from his shoulder. As she did so, Slim reached up and gently grabbed her wrist. Lori stopped and looked down at him.

"Lori." It was the first time he had ever used her name. "Thanks."

That was all. "Thanks." Lori looked at Slim for a moment and then just nodded. He let go of her wrist, and she walked out of the room. She came up to where I stood and stopped, realizing I had been watching. A little color came to her face. No words were needed, though, and she just smiled, nodded, and walked away.

That was one of the last times I saw Slim. He died a few years ago. Yet I remember this particular ER visit well, and Lori's unflinching care for the man. This had been more than just doing her job. It was a manifestation of her spirit and her selflessness. I've tried to respond more like Lori when I find myself in similar circumstances. Sometimes I succeed. Sometimes I don't. But when I don't succeed, when I back away from an unpleasant circumstance or a patient who is less than attractive, I at least realize my shortcoming. Maybe that's the first step.

> *The King will reply, "I tell you the truth, whatever you did for one of the least of these brothers of mine, you did for me."*
>
> —MATTHEW 25:40

3

A **Turn** in the **Road**

*For a little while you may have had to suffer grief
in all kinds of trials. These have come so that your
faith—of greater worth than gold, which perishes even
though refined by fire—may be proved genuine.*

—1 PETER 1:6-7

It seemed like a simple thing. Frank and Katie Giles were on their way from Cleveland to Myrtle Beach, South Carolina, traveling southbound on I-77 when it happened. They had driven this road many times in the past—in fact, each year for the past fifteen. Two of their best friends had moved to the beach years earlier, and the annual trek had become a tradition. Also, it was a chance for the Giles to take a vacation as winter was reluctantly beginning to lose its grip on the Ohio Valley. Frank had just turned sixty-six and had retired a few months ago, so this would be the first time they would be able to spend two full weeks at the beach with their friends.

It had seemed innocent enough, a trivial thing. They were still in North Carolina, negotiating the last remnants of morning rush-hour traffic in Charlotte, and Katie had asked Frank if he wanted her to drive for a while.

When he didn't respond, she looked up from the magazine she was reading and repeated her question. "Frank, you've been driving for almost two hours. Do you want me to take over?"

His hands gripped the wheel perhaps a little too tightly, and he stared straight ahead. She studied his face for a moment. His eyes were tracking the busy and unpredictable traffic surrounding them, and he was handling the van without any problem. And yet there was something wrong. His eyebrows were raised anxiously, something unusual for him, and his lips were trembling, as if trying to form a word or a sound.

"Frank?" Katie said, now worried. She reached over and touched his arm.

And then it was over. Just like that. It had been only half a minute, maybe a little less.

"Wha…" he stammered, shaking his head as if to clear it. "What did you say, Katie? Do I want you to drive? No, no, I'm fine," he answered, now more relaxed.

She continued to search his face, relieved by what he had just said. But she was still concerned, and the uneasy feeling was only slowly beginning to fade.

"Whew, Frank. You had me worried there. You must have been daydreaming." She put her magazine in the passenger-door pocket.

He straightened his arms out, pressing himself back in the seat.

"That was really weird," he began. "I could hear you talking plain as day, and I could see everything going on around us. But I couldn't say anything. I knew what I wanted to say but I couldn't make myself say it. My mouth wouldn't work. Darnedest thing that's ever happened to me."

"Frank, are you alright now?" Katie asked, her anxiety returning.

"I'm fine now," he responded, realizing he needed to calm his wife. "I just couldn't talk, just for a second. No headache, no nothing. I'm fine. Honest." He patted his wife's knee as they sped down the highway.

She looked intently at her husband of forty years. He seemed all right. He was his normal self now, making sense, and he seemed in control of his faculties. Yet something like that shouldn't happen. She just knew it.

She was silent for a few miles and then said, "Frank, we need to stop and see a doctor."

He jerked his head to look at her. "What? I'm fine, Katie. Honest. We don't need to stop anywhere, and I don't need to see a doctor."

"No, we're going to stop. It's still several hours to Myrtle Beach and I won't feel right unless we have you checked out."

She was sitting bolt upright, her arms folded across her chest. He was very familiar with this posture and knew her mind was made up. They passed a mileage sign, and she said, "Look, Rock Hill is just ten miles away. We'll stop there. That's a good-sized town, and they'll have a hospital. We'll just follow the signs."

And then she was silent. Frank knew this silence, and knew that it would do no good to try to dissuade her. They would stop in Rock Hill and find a hospital.

The process begins. Someone punches your ticket, hands it back to you, and then you're on the train. There's no stopping. And just as when you've boarded a train, you have no control over where the process is heading. It's almost as if it has a mind of its own.

It's often a simple thing—an innocent-appearing symptom, a seemingly meaningless change in the way you feel, an unexpected finding in a routine examination. You go to your doctor or to the ER to have this "new thing" checked out. One examination, one test leads to another. Something else turns up. "We need to look into this further." Or the unwelcome words, "We're going to need to have you see a specialist."

When the pretense of self-determination and control is stripped away, when the flimsy, artificial layers we construct for our protection are gone, it is our mortality that stares us in the face. Almost daily, one of the staff members in the ER will utter the phrase, "I don't know how they can stand that. What will they do?" It is posed as a rhetorical question, and goes unanswered. But the dark thought hangs in the air. It sobers us for a moment, strikes a chord that is both familiar and uncomfortable. *There but for fortune…* And then we move on.

Not so for the person holding the ticket.

Frank was sitting up in room 2. He was in a hospital gown and seemed embarrassed as he struggled with the tie strings behind him. Katie was trying to help. She clucked as she shook her head. "Why do they always make these things so short?"

"They do, don't they?" I said, entering the room and pulling the curtain closed behind me. "Hi, I'm Dr. Lesslie. What can we do for you this morning?"

They both looked up. Katie had managed to knot the strings and secure Frank's gown.

"Hello, Doctor," Frank began. "I'm not sure I even need to be here, but my wife—"

Katie quickly interrupted. "His wife is concerned about him and wants him evaluated. We're on vacation, and Frank had an unusual episode a little while ago while we were driving on the interstate. I just want him to be checked out."

She went on to explain the brief problem her husband had experienced. Frank sat leaning forward on the stretcher, his arms folded and his head down.

When she had finished, I asked Frank how he felt now and what he remembered of the incident.

"Doc, I feel fine now, completely normal," he responded. "And about what happened on the road, it was just really unusual. I could hear Katie, and I knew what I wanted to say, but I couldn't make my mouth work. It was strange. And then it passed and was gone."

He seemed fine now, but the story was bothersome. He might have had a small stroke, or he might have an aneurysm that was beginning to leak. His heart could be throwing out tiny clots. This could represent a number of potentially serious things, or it could be just a passing problem, one that would never recur.

His physical examination was completely normal. His vital signs were also within normal limits, his neurological status was fine, and his cardiac exam was okay. But something just didn't seem right, and the fact they were on the road, headed away from home, bothered me.

"Well, everything looks good now, but I think we should just check things out a little more. What I would recommend is that we get a CT scan of your head and make sure there are no problems there," I explained.

"Dr. Lesslie, I—" Frank began.

But Katie interrupted him again, patting him on the arm. "Dr. Lesslie, you go ahead and do what you think needs to be done. I want to be sure everything is alright before we head on to Myrtle Beach."

Frank looked up at her, and an expression of mild consternation gave way to one of resignation.

I looked at him, seeking his approval.

"Well…okay, Doc. If that's what you think is best."

"I do, Mr. Giles. It should only take an hour or so, and when we get the results we should be able to send you on your way. I'll just feel better about things if I know the scan is normal."

"We'll feel better too, Doctor. And thank you," Katie responded, smiling.

The Radiology Department was adjacent to the ER, just around the corner. Fortunately the CT machines were not too busy this morning. They were able to get Mr. Giles in right away, and in thirty minutes to an hour or so I would get a faxed report from the radiologist. As I stood at the nurses' station writing on his record, I didn't anticipate a bad outcome. I knew I was being cautious, maybe overly so. But with people from out of town who are just passing through, you tended to be a little extra careful. Most of our patients are from Rock Hill, or from within the county. And most have family physicians they can see in the next day or two for follow-up if needed. And if they get worse, they can always come back to the ER. But for those who are traveling, you want to be sure you aren't sending them down the road with a problem that has not been identified or resolved.

The department had gotten busier while I had been in room 2 with the Gileses. I had taken care of a sore throat, started the workup of an elderly man with abdominal pain, and taken a quick look at a lacerated finger, when I saw Frank Giles being wheeled back into the department by two X-ray techs, his wife walking by his side. They were smiling at me as they were taken to his room.

I was talking to Amy, requesting some lab studies for the gentleman with abdominal pain. "We'll need a CBC, electrolytes, amylase, lipase, and an obstructive series for room 3, if you can get that going. Oh, and see if you can find a family member. He's not able to tell me too much."

"Sure thing," Amy responded. She'd anticipated this and had already notified the X-ray techs.

Frank Giles's chart was on the counter, and I noticed there was no faxed report attached to it. Usually the report would beat the patient back to the department. I glanced at the fax machine that sat at Amy's elbow. Nothing.

Then the phone rang.

Amy picked up the receiver while continuing to fill out the lab requests for the patient in room 3.

"ER," she answered. "Ms. Conners speaking."

There was a brief pause, and then, "Sure, he's standin' right here, Dr. Stringer. Let me give him the phone."

"It's for you," she said, handing me the receiver without looking up from her paperwork. "Dr. Stringer in Radiology."

Matt Stringer had joined the Radiology staff a little over two years ago. He had extensive training in neuroradiology and, just as important, he was easy to work with. He seemed to understand the pressures we were under in the ER, and he never tried to second-guess us when we ordered studies, especially requests made in the middle of the night. He would frequently walk over to our department with films he thought were especially noteworthy, and together we would go over them. He had taught me a lot about the rapidly changing technologies of scanning and the newer forms of imaging.

"Hey, Matt," I spoke into the phone. "What's going on?"

"Robert, this Mr. Giles you sent over for a CT scan, what can you tell me about him?" The tone of Matt's voice was all business, something unusual for him.

"Well, what do you mean? From a neurological standpoint he's fine. He had a brief episode earlier this morning of expressive aphasia, but that resolved and he's been fine since. Why, what do you see on his scan?" I asked, becoming concerned. This should have been straightforward, a normal and perfunctory report. Apparently it was not.

"You mean he hasn't had any problems before today?" Matt questioned. "No headaches, imbalance, change in behavior?"

"No. Not that he or his wife told me about. Why?"

Matt paused and then said, "You'd better come over to the department and take a look at this scan with me."

"I'll be right there."

I told Amy where I would be and glanced briefly at room 2, where the curtain was pulled open. The Gileses were quietly talking to each other and didn't look in my direction. I turned and walked down the hall toward the back of the ER and then to Radiology.

Matt Stringer was in one of the viewing rooms, sitting in a black leather chair. He was studying a row of films attached to a light box. He pressed a button and with a soft mechanical groan, the row moved upward and an entirely new set of films came into view.

"Hey, Matt," I greeted him, stepping into the dimly lighted cubicle. "What do you have?"

I stepped behind him, leaned over his right shoulder, and looked at the view box. He was reaching out his hand and pointing to one of the X-rays, but my eyes had already found his intended target. I was stunned.

"Take a look at that, Robert," he said, gently tapping the film. In front of us was a CT scan, a cross section of Frank Giles's skull and brain. And in the middle of what should have been normal brain matter was something that shouldn't have been there. The size of a tennis ball, it was clearly demarcated, being a different shade of gray from the surrounding tissue. The ominous-appearing mass had extended its tentacles into Frank's defenseless cerebrum.

I knew at once what it was, but I asked Matt anyway, hoping I was wrong. "What do you think that is?"

"It has to be a glioblastoma. And pretty aggressive, from the looks of it," he answered. "And you say this guy hasn't been having any symptoms? Look at the size of this thing. That would be hard to believe."

I continued to stare at the X-ray, and my mind raced. *A brain tumor.* How was I going to break this to the Gileses? What was I going to tell them?

"No, Matt. I asked both of them repeatedly, and he has been doing great. No headaches, no visual changes, no weight loss, no gait disturbance. Nothing. Just that brief episode this morning," I told him. It didn't seem logical to me, either. This was a huge tumor and it occupied a lot of space. You would think from its size and location it would have announced itself by now.

"Hmm," Matt mused. "Well, it doesn't really matter, does it? This thing is going to kill him. It's too big and too invasive to do anything with. It's in a terrible location and it must be growing pretty fast. Does this guy live here in town?"

I told Matt of the circumstances in which the Gileses found themselves. He rubbed his chin and looked up at me. "Good luck, Robert. I don't envy you having to tell them about this."

I wasn't feeling so good about it myself. "Well, thanks, Matt. I guess I'd better get back to the ER and sit down with these folks."

"Okay, I'll see you later. Let me know if I can do anything." He turned back to his work and pressed the button on the desktop. With the same quiet mechanical groan, the films from Frank Giles's CT scan disappeared from view, and the X-rays of someone else's life took their place.

The walk back to the ER was long but not long enough. The fact that I didn't know these people wouldn't make this any easier. They were good folks, and they would immediately understand the implications of what I had to tell them.

Virginia Granger was standing at the nurses' station as I approached. She looked up from the legal pad she had in her hand and took off her glasses. Tapping the pad with them, she said, "Dr. Lesslie, there are a couple of things we need to go over before we have our staff meeting in the morning. Do you have a few minutes now, or would another time be better?"

I picked up Frank Giles's chart from the countertop. "How about later, Virginia? I need to take care of a few things right now."

She put her glasses back on and studied my face, her head canted to one side. "Are you alright? Is there a problem?"

Glancing in the direction of the Gileses' room, I noted that the curtain was pulled closed. "I've got some bad news for the people in room 2, and it will take a few minutes." I briefly told her what I had just learned.

Virginia pursed her lips, nodded her head slightly, and said, "Why don't I go in there with you? Maybe I can help."

I looked up from Frank's chart and into her eyes. They were a steely gray. What most people found cold and intimidating, I found compassionate and incisive. Her years in the military and in the ER had tempered this compassion with an edge of reserve, but had not defeated it. And I knew she had delivered equally devastating news to too many people like Frank and Katie Giles.

I appreciated her offer, and for a moment considered taking her up on it. "No—but thanks, Virginia," I told her. "I'd better just do this myself."

Katie stood at the head of the stretcher, her hand resting on her husband's shoulder. They looked up as I came into the room. I pulled the curtain closed behind me and sat down on the stool that stood against the wall. There was an expectant look on their faces, and the traces of a smile on Katie's. Frank sat stiffly, the fingers of his hands interlocked and resting in his lap.

What should I say? How was I going to begin this? And then Katie helped me. "Well, what have you found, Doctor? Is everything all right? Can we resume our trip?"

I held Frank's chart against my chest and leaned forward.

"Frank, Katie, I'm afraid I have some bad news."

She tensed, and her hand, which had been gently resting on his shoulder, now gripped it tightly. Her eyes widened.

"The CT scan was not normal. There's a problem."

"What kind of problem?" Katie asked, insistently. "What's the matter?"

Frank was silent.

"Frank, I'm afraid you have a brain tumor."

Katie gasped, and her hand went to her mouth.

The color drained from Frank's face. "A brain tumor?" he echoed. There was a brief pause. "How bad is it, Dr. Lesslie?"

This was something I could handle, a clinical question. This was familiar and more comfortable turf.

"First, I'm not a neurosurgeon," I explained. "But this thing is pretty large. It's in a bad location and it looks aggressive."

"What does that mean?" he asked.

"The radiologist that looked at your scan thinks it is most likely a certain type of tumor that grows quickly. One that's not going to do well."

There was silence for a moment, and then Katie spoke. "And what does that mean?"

"Again, Mrs. Giles, I'm not a neurosurgeon. But this is a bad problem. And it's something that needs to be taken care of, as soon as possible."

"No, what I want to know is—" she persisted, but her husband patted her on her arm and interrupted her.

"Doctor, what do you think we should do? What should we do right now? Do you think it's safe to go on to Myrtle Beach, or should we just head back home?" he asked me.

I had already thought about this, and I told him what I would do in this circumstance. "My advice would be to cancel your trip and head back home. You're going to need to see your personal physician, and together you can decide how you want to proceed with this. The episode this morning was something small, but I'm afraid something worse could happen at any time. I think it will be safe for you to travel—but Mrs. Giles, I would advise that you do the driving."

Katie had tears in her eyes, and she nodded her head.

"But what about our friends at the beach?" he asked, looking up at her. "They'll be expecting us this afternoon."

Katie was silent.

I stood up. "Why don't the two of you talk this over for a few minutes? If you decide to go on to Myrtle Beach, I will call down there and see if I can arrange for some help if you should need it. Whatever you decide, you'll need to take a copy of your CT scan with you, and I'll arrange for that. I'll be back in a couple of minutes."

Pulling the curtain closed behind me, I walked over and sat down beside Amy. I was drained.

The couple of minutes turned into half an hour as the elderly gentleman with abdominal pain demanded my attention. His X-rays revealed that he had perforated his large intestine and would need the services of a surgeon. When this had been arranged, I stepped back into room 2 to check on the Gileses.

The atmosphere of the room had been dark and oppressive when I left. Now it had completely changed. He was dressed, and they were both standing by the bed, their arms around each other's waists. And they were smiling.

Frank was the first to speak. "We've decided to take your advice and we're going to head back home. We'll need to make a few phone calls and then we can be on our way."

It was Katie's turn. "And we want to thank you for your help, Dr. Lesslie," she told me. "This has certainly been a surprise, and not what we ever wanted to hear. But it is what it is, and we needed to know about it."

I just stood there and listened.

"Katie's right, Doctor. And we'll handle this. We'll be all right with whatever comes our way."

There was a pause, and I was just about to turn from the room when Frank continued. "We are spiritual people, doctor. Not religious, necessarily. There's a difference, you know."

A movement from Katie drew my attention. It was then that I

noticed the small silver cross that hung by a chain from her neck. Her hand had gone to the cross, and she clutched it gently.

"I'm not an old man, by any means. Or at least I don't feel old," Frank chuckled. "But I've had a lot of good years and we've done a lot of good things. If this thing, this tumor, is a bad one and it can't be fixed—well, then, so be it. And if I thought this life, these few years we have on this earth, were all that are given us—well, I suppose I would have something to be upset about. But that's not what we believe. This is just the first part, the first step. And I'm okay with this thing. We're okay."

Katie looked up at her husband and smiled, then pressed herself closer to him.

Standing at the nurses' station, I was finishing the work on Frank Giles's chart as Virginia Granger led him and his wife out through triage. His eye caught mine and he gave me a nod of his head, and then, amazingly, a wink. Then the couple disappeared behind the closing door. They were beginning a new and unexpected journey.

Frank's ticket had been punched. He was on his train, and Katie was with him. Wherever that train was headed, they would be on it together. And I sensed that wherever the journey ended, they would be okay.

I have set the LORD always before me. Because he
is at my right hand, I will not be shaken.

—PSALM 16:8

4

All **God's Children**

Every man naturally desires knowledge; but what good
is knowledge without fear of God? Indeed a humble
rustic who serves God is better than a proud intellectual
who neglects his soul to study the course of the stars.

—Thomas à Kempis

One universal truth is that the ER is the great leveler of personages. We reach a common ground and find ourselves dealing with the same problems as everyone else around us: pain and suffering, health and disease, and sometimes life and death. At that point, our addresses make no difference, nor do our titles and degrees, nor do the quality and purchase price of the clothes we wear.

Another infallible truth of life in the emergency room is that just as soon as you believe you are good at what you do, that you are capable of handling anything thrown at you, at that moment or in the not-too-distant future, you will be brought low. We have to learn not to take ourselves too seriously and to get our egos out of the way so we can be useful to others. This is the case not only for those of us who work in the ER. As it turns out, this is a challenge just as much for the patients, no matter what their walk in life.

❧

2:15 p.m. It was a Tuesday afternoon, mid-May, and the weather outside was beautiful. It had been a manageable day thus far, and the staff was in good spirits. Lori Davidson was working triage. She opened the door out of that area and brought Mrs. Betty Booth out into the department, leading her toward the observation room.

As they passed the nurses' station, Amy Conners looked up from behind the counter.

"Good afternoon, Mrs. Booth," she said, smiling at the elderly woman.

"Good afternoon, Amy," Mrs. Booth responded, nodding her head but not returning the smile. "I hope my room is clean and ready," she added.

It wasn't exactly *her* room, but maybe it should have been. She had been coming to the ER each afternoon for three weeks to receive special medication for a bone-marrow condition. Her doctor had ordered that it be given intravenously, and the process took about two hours. During that time she would be our guest in one of the observation-room beds. At this time of day, these beds were seldom used, and she usually had a moderate degree of privacy.

"I'm sure everything is ready for you," Amy responded, rolling her eyes for my benefit once Lori and our guest had passed by.

Mrs. Betty Booth was a pillar of the community, as had been her family for several generations. Her lineage was dotted with a few mayors, city councilmen, and even a state senator. She was a widow now, with no children, and she represented the last vestiges of "old Rock Hill." This appellation was important to her and she wanted to be sure that those who attended her understood it. She was very demanding about her care and surroundings. She brooked neither inattentiveness nor any avoidable disruption of her established routine. We had suggested she come to the ER in the early afternoons, as this was usually our quietest time. Still, it was an ER. We couldn't guarantee peace and tranquility, even in the observation room.

On this particular day, she would be alone in OBS. The room was clean, quiet, and she would be able to choose her own stretcher.

"I'd like to be over in that bed," she instructed Lori, pointing to the back right corner of the room—bed C. "And make sure that the curtains are drawn."

Lori dutifully helped Mrs. Booth onto the stretcher, raised the head to a comfortable level, and gave her a blanket straight from the warmer.

"Your nurse will be with you in a moment to start your IV," she told her. "I'll need to go back out to triage now."

"That will be fine, Lori. And make sure you tell her not to dawdle."

Lori walked out of the room and over to the nurses' station.

"Who's got OBS today?" she asked, glancing at the assignment board.

Virginia Granger was sitting at the nurses' station, working on one of her administrative reports. "Becka's got it, Lori, but she's on break right now. Give me the chart and I'll get things started. I know Mrs. Booth."

Amy handed her the chart and headed back to triage.

Becka Hemby was twenty-two years old and a recent graduate from the local nursing program. She had been in the ER for only about a month. Though she had the potential to be a good ER nurse, she was still learning the ropes.

Within a few minutes, Virginia had Betty's IV started and had ordered her medication from the pharmacy. It would be delivered shortly. Mrs. Booth was reclining comfortably, reading her *Southern Living* magazine behind her closed curtains. Everything seemed to be on schedule.

And then things turned south. It seems to happen that way, doesn't it? Just when everything seems under control, rolling along smoothly, there's a sudden bump in the road—and then a pothole.

The bump in the road came in the form of our young nurse, Miss Hemby. She had come back from her break and gone out to relieve Lori in triage. All routine. Lori would be back in fifteen minutes and Becka would resume her regular assignment, which included the observation room. It was those fifteen minutes that would prove to be crucial. That's when the pothole arrived, in the person of Jasper Little.

Jasper was one of our regulars. He had a predilection for MD

20/20 and would frequently consume it to the point of oblivion. This was an unusual time of day for him to appear in the department. His blood alcohol level usually didn't reach the customary .40 range until later in the evening. But someone had given him ten dollars to help with an odd job and he had headed straight to his favorite store.

Becka greeted Mr. Little and took him into triage. There she obtained his vital signs and tried to make some sense out of what he was saying. He could barely walk, and he seemed to be speaking something other than English. She made a wise decision to place him in a wheelchair and rolled him into the department. She rightly assumed Jasper would need some fluids and medications, and she glanced at the board at the nurses' station to determine the most appropriate room. In her brief time with us, she had helped take care of him during one of his bouts with the DTs.

Hmm, she thought. *OBS has only one patient, Jasper'll probably be with us for a while, so I'll take him there.*

She rolled Jasper into OBS and over to the stretcher of bed B, in the back left corner of the room. Mrs. Booth was contentedly reading behind her curtain, unaware of her new roommate.

Just then, Lori came back from her break. She stuck her head in OBS and told Becka she was headed out to triage, and she took Jasper's wheelchair with her. She didn't look up to see the identity of the new patient.

Becka busied herself with Mr. Little. It was no small task to get him up on the stretcher and secure him behind the raised rails. She knew department policy and got him undressed to his underwear and into a hospital gown.

"You stay right here, Mr. Little," she instructed him. "I'll be right back."

He mumbled a response that was completely unintelligible and then lay back on the bed and closed his eyes.

I happened to be the one who picked up Jasper's chart when it hit the counter. I assumed that this would be a routine visit: IV fluids, multivitamins and thiamine through his IV line, and observation for several hours. We would get a blood alcohol on him and put together a pool to see who could come the closest without going over. Briefly, the thought crossed my mind that he probably shouldn't be in OBS with Mrs. Booth. She considered it her private domain, and she certainly didn't travel in the same circles as Jasper Little. Nevertheless, he was already bedded down, and what was the worst that could happen?

We found out in about an hour. Becka had checked on Mrs. Booth and made sure she was comfortable. Her medication was infusing smoothly and she should be ready to go home in thirty minutes or so. Becka then stepped across to Jasper's stretcher.

"Mr. Little," she said, gently shaking his shoulder. "How are you doing?"

He raised his head off the pillow and half opened his eyes. "Gotta pee," he declared.

"Excuse me?" Becka asked.

"Gotta pee," he repeated. His head fell back on the pillow and his eyes again closed.

She looked at his IV line. It was running wide open and he had already received almost two liters of fluids. *He probably does have to urinate,* she thought.

She glanced at the counter behind the stretcher and didn't see a urinal or bedpan. She was concerned that Jasper was still too unsteady on his feet to get him up and walk him to the bathroom.

"I understand, Mr. Little," she told him. "I'm going to step out for just a second and get a urinal for you. I'll be right back."

"Gotta pee," he mumbled.

I was at the nurses' station when Becka came out of OBS and headed for the supply closet. She was in there for several minutes before sticking her head out and asking, "Does anyone know where the urinals are kept?"

Before anyone could respond, there came a loud shriek from OBS. It was Mrs. Booth. "Oh, good Lord! Somebody help me!"

Becka bolted out of the supply closet and headed for OBS. I put down the chart I was holding and followed her.

"Somebody help! Do something!"

When I reached the doorway, Becka was pulling aside Mrs. Booth's curtain and asking, "Mrs. Booth, what's the…"

She stopped in mid-sentence and just stared.

Betty Booth sat bolt upright in her bed, her hands covering her mouth and her eyes wide as saucers. Then with one hand she pointed to the foot of her bed.

There in all his glory stood Jasper Little. He had somehow gotten out of his stretcher and walked across the room, IV pole in tow. Becka had put his gown on backward, so the opening was in the front. He stood at the foot of Mrs. Booth's bed with his hands on his hips, eyes closed, and pelvis thrust forward. He was relieving himself on the end of her stretcher, and he was doing so with unrestrained enthusiasm.

"Gotta pee," he mumbled, smiling and nodding his head.

Becka quickly pulled the curtain closed and led Jasper back to his bed. Mrs. Booth remained speechless, shaken to the core. The next day, her physician arranged for another facility to administer her medication. We haven't seen her since.

❦

10:15 p.m. Two police officers escorted a middle-aged man into the department.

"Good evenin', Doc," one of them greeted me as they approached the nurses' station. "Got some business for you."

I glanced up and nodded hello, barely noticing the man between them. He was handcuffed, his hair tousled and his shirt partway out of his pants. I glanced down at his feet and noticed he wore only one shoe. Then I looked at his face again and realized he looked familiar. My index finger went to my chin and my head cocked to one side as I struggled for his name.

Then it came to me. The look of recognition on my face must have been obvious, because the officer who had spoken nodded his head and said, "Yep, got a VIP for you here."

The shackled visitor didn't seem to hear this. I'm not sure he was hearing much of anything. He reeked of alcohol, and his slouching posture and lolling head indicated he had passed way beyond being "under the influence."

Jeff Ryan had walked up to the counter. "Go ahead and take him back to ortho," he instructed the officers. "There's no one in there and he should be out of the way."

"Sure thing," they responded and headed down the hallway. They knew their way around the department as well as we did.

When they were a safe distance away, Jeff said, "Now isn't that somethin'?"

"Isn't that Joe Sightler?" I asked. "The mayor of Hazelton?" This was a small town about twenty minutes outside of Rock Hill. He was a high-profile local politician, frequently in the news, and never one to shy away from controversial issues.

"That's Joe alright," Jeff answered. "Looks like he's in a bit of a pickle tonight."

"Or at least pickled," Amy punned from behind the desk. "He can barely stand."

This should be interesting, I thought. I had some other work to do, and it would take a while for his chart to make its way to the counter. Still, it was going to be interesting.

Every emergency department has had its share of VIP patients. We've had movie actors, professional football players, politicians, and professional wrestlers. Even famous biblical characters—I once took care of a man who claimed to be John the Baptist. They all get treated the same and are shown no favoritism, nor do they receive any special perks. (We did keep a close eye on John, though. He was a little different.) The fact is, we all put our pants on one leg at a time. We all have the same weaknesses and maladies, the same needs and the same quandaries. Joe Sightler might be a well-known politician, but in this ER on this night, he was just a man in need of medical attention. I wasn't exactly sure what that attention was going to be, but it didn't look like it would be anything serious. He would be in line just like everyone else.

I picked up his chart from the countertop just as one of his police officers walked up.

"Mr. Sightler was involved in a fender bender," he told me. "Actually, I'm not sure it even qualifies as a fender bender. He was at a local restaurant this evening and had a few too many to drink. We were stopped at a red light right beside the restaurant when he came out and got in his car. We sat through the next green light and just watched, 'cause we couldn't believe what we were seeing. He barely made it across the parking lot without falling. We thought, *No way is this guy gonna try to drive!*"

The officer stopped and shook his head, still unable to believe what had happened. Then he continued. "We pulled into the lot and tried to stop him, but before we could, he gunned the motor and backed right into a light post. I guess he couldn't see the post, 'cause he kept rammin' into it. Hit it a couple of times. I had to reach in and cut off the motor."

When he paused this time, I glanced down at Joe's chart and searched for "chief complaint." The business office had typed in, "Auto accident. No complaints. Police request blood alcohol."

"Let me go check him out," I told the officer. "And we'll get you guys out of here as quickly as we can."

"No hurry, Doc. Our shift's almost over. We'll take Joe down to the station, and it looks like he'll be spending at least tonight with us. I guess we'll be in the paper in the morning."

"Probably so," I agreed.

After checking Joe out and determining he had no significant physical injury, we awaited his blood alcohol. He had agreed to have it drawn, having slurred, "I don't have anything to hide."

My guess was it was going to be north of .40.

This wasn't the first time, unfortunately, we had taken care of the mayor in an inebriated condition. You'd think he would have practiced some discretion with his use of alcohol, but he seemed oblivious to the potential repercussions. Or maybe he assumed he was above any public reprimand or ballyhoo.

As I walked back up the hall, a momentary lull in our overhead music caught my attention. Our automatic CD changer was located in the doctor's office and we were able to select the music in the ER. Within a few seconds, sounds from Motown drifted through the department. I recognized the voices of the Temptations as they began "My Girl."

Standing at the nurses' station, I was handed a lab slip from the fax. It revealed Joe Sightler's blood alcohol: .465, more than four times the legal limit.

"That should about do it," the officer remarked, looking over my shoulder.

"I guess he's all yours," I told him. "We'll have him ready to go in just a few minutes."

It was then that the universally familiar rhythm at the beginning of "I Heard It Through the Grapevine" wafted through the department.

"Good tune," the officer remarked, his head rocking in time to the song.

Mr. Sightler must have heard the music as well. An unexpected movement down the hallway caught my attention and I looked in the direction of the doorway of the ortho room. Joe was out of the room and walking up the hallway. You couldn't exactly call it walking. He was still in his hospital gown, barefooted. His hands were raised shoulder-high, palms facing forward, and he was doing a kind of shimmy motion. His eyes were closed and his head rocked from side to side.

"Ooooo, ooooo, I bet you're wonderin' how I knew…" he crooned. Actually, his pitch was pretty good.

Two radiology techs turned the corner behind him. They were pushing a wheelchair with an elderly woman in it. She had injured her ankle and we had sent her around for an X-ray. The three were met by the stately mayoral vision as he meandered up the hall. Only their view was a little different from ours. Joe's gown was open in the back and untied. His underwear was hanging on a hook somewhere. And his behind was gloriously exposed to the whole world.

The woman in the wheelchair seemed to appreciate it. Though we heard a faint yelp and saw her cover her eyes, she continued to peek between her spread fingers. The radiology techs just smiled. They had seen quite a few hineys before. Heads began popping out from behind curtains and people got to see one of their elected officials up close and personal.

"Mm-hmm," the officer murmured. "Would you look at that."

I supposed the mayor would have kept on dancing right out of the department if we'd let him. But maybe not. When he neared the nurses' station he stopped, opened one eye, looked in my direction, and winked.

The officers led him back down the hall and helped him get dressed. One leg at a time.

When pride comes, then comes disgrace, but
with humility comes wisdom.

—Proverbs 11:2

5

The **Experience** of **Grief**

*Although the world is full of suffering, it is
also full of the overcoming of it.*

—HELEN KELLER (1880–1968)

G rief. We are told that as humans our handling of grief or loss
can be logically and predictably chronicled through four distinct
phases. First there is shock, followed by denial, then anger, and finally
resolution.

All griefs and losses, major and minor, work the same way. We
travel through the phases, backing up, retracing our steps, making
progress again, relapsing, and on it goes. The ability to reach resolution
and stay there is a gift, a thing for which we ought to be grateful.

For most of us, this final resolution is a rare occurrence. Our natu-
ral inclination is to travel in circles, not in a straight line. And these
circles can be destructive. Shock, denial, anger. Shock, denial, anger.
Never reaching resolution.

Every day in the ER we see people faced with small griefs, and many
times with overwhelming losses. We watch as they come to grips with
their emotions and deal with sudden and unexpected life-changing
events. Sometimes we can help. Often, we can't. I have found that you
can frequently predict how people will respond in crisis. Over the years
you gain a sense of who seems grounded and in control of their emotions. And who is not. You can usually identify that person who is only
one word, one whisper, one sideways glance away from totally losing it.
Many times you will be correct, but not always. Sometimes the actions
and reactions of people will take you completely by surprise.

◈

I had been working in the ER of Rock Hill General for a few years. On this particular Sunday morning about twenty years ago, one of my partners, Bill Blanchard, had been on duty in the department. It was a beautiful morning—springtime, quiet, nonthreatening. The ER was peaceful. At 9:30, Bill was having his second cup of coffee and was reading the local newspaper. There were only a handful of nonemergent patients remaining from a brief rush at sunrise and Virginia Granger, the charge nurse that day, was discharging one of them. She passed through the nurses' station where Bill sat with his paper in one hand and his cup of coffee in the other. His feet were casually occupying the countertop.

As Virginia passed by she paused, looked over the top of her glasses at his shoes, and simply said, "Dr. Blanchard."

He didn't need a second warning.

"Oh, excuse me," he responded, coming to an upright position in his chair with his feet firmly located on the floor. He kept his head in the newspaper, not looking up as he ceded this turf to Virginia. It was an act born out of respect more than out of intimidation, though Virginia had quite a menacing reputation in the hospital, especially among new physicians. She brooked no tomfoolery in her department.

But Bill was no intern, having completed his training in emergency medicine in a large urban medical center eight years earlier. He had been in this particular hospital for more than six years and was a seasoned ER doc. He was one of the favorites of the occasional medical student or intern who rotated through the department because he was always accessible for their many elementary questions. "What's the dose of amoxicillin for a two-year-old?" "Does 'TID' mean twice a day or three times a day?" "I think this guy in room 5 has pink eye. What should I treat him with?"

I never saw him demonstrate any impatience, even when one

befuddled intern confronted him with, "Dr. Blanchard, I've got a guy here I think has appendicitis. Now, I know the appendix is on the right side, but is it *his* right or *my* right, and does it depend on which way I'm facing him?"

"Hmm," Bill had calmly responded, with an air of appropriate but feigned seriousness so as not to embarrass this fledgling physician. "I suppose that would be *his* right, wouldn't it?"

He was a steadying influence for each of us and shared freely of his practical and varied experience.

Yet he was about to teach all of us one of his most important lessons, though not by intent or design. And it was certainly not of his own choosing.

This particular morning Bill was the only physician in the ER. He moved on to the sports section of the paper, taking advantage of the rare respite.

Virginia had noted his reposturing, with both of his feet now firmly on the floor. She acknowledged her approval with a slight nod and proceeded toward her patient's room. She was interrupted by the high-pitched squawk of the EMS radio.

"ER, this is Medic 1. Do you read me?"

Bill casually looked up from his paper as Virginia put down her chart and walked over to the radio. Having done this thousands of times, she matter-of-factly took out her pen, picked up the phone, and prepared to make notes on the pad of paper beside the radio.

"This is the General ER, Medic 1. Go ahead."

There was silence and then a brief burst of static.

"ER, we're out on the interstate with a 10-50 (auto accident). Two PIs (personal injuries), one dead at the scene. The other looks okay. Twenty-five-year-old male. We're bringing him in on a backboard, full spinal protocol. Ten minutes away."

"10-4, Medic 1. Minor trauma 3 on arrival," Virginia instructed the paramedic. She finished her notations and picked up her chart, once more trying to discharge her patient.

Bill spoke over his newspaper to her. "Sounds like a bad accident. A little unusual for a Sunday morning."

"Yeah," Virginia answered. "But you never know. People do strange things."

Ten minutes later, the ambulance entrance doors opened to admit a stretcher being pushed by one of the hospital's paramedics. His partner EMT steadied the side of the gurney. Their patient was strapped securely to a backboard, head held firmly to it by Velcro straps.

From the nurses' station Bill could get enough of a glimpse of the young man to determine he was in no immediate danger. The patient's eyes darted to and fro and he kept asking, "Where is my wife? How is she?"

The EMT pushed the stretcher into minor trauma and the paramedic walked over to the nurses' station, clipboard in hand. He approached Bill, leaned over, and quietly spoke. "Dr. Blanchard, this is really a tough one." He tilted his head down the hallway toward this newest patient.

"Young couple, got married yesterday somewhere in Tennessee. Spent the night just north of town and were on their way to the beach for their honeymoon. An eighteen-wheeler changed lanes in front of them, and this guy swerved and lost control. Flipped over twice. The girl didn't have a seat belt on and was thrown out of the car and down an embankment. Pretty bad head injury. Looked like she died on impact. He hardly has a scratch on him."

The paramedic stood up straight, put his hands on the small of his back, and stretched.

"Does he have any idea what happened to his wife?" Bill asked him.

"No, not a clue. We didn't say anything. And the highway patrolman wouldn't tell him. I guess you get to," he added sheepishly.

"Yeah, well, I guess so," Bill conceded. He had been in this position too many times before.

Virginia worked efficiently, and within half an hour Bill had cleared the young man, Mr. Jones, of any significant injury. In fact, he had no complaints and had only noticed a few scratches on his left hand. He continued to ask about his wife, and Bill deftly avoided any specific response. He was awaiting the arrival of the highway patrolman to confirm the story given him by the paramedic.

Bill walked past the young man's room and noticed he was up and off the stretcher, standing by the gurney. His hands were in his pockets and he was quietly staring at the doorway. Virginia had just told him that as soon as they had definite news about his wife they would share that information with him.

When Bill reached the nurses' station he said, "Virginia, why don't you take him to the family room. Try to keep him calm, and I'll be in there in a few minutes."

"Okay, I'll try," she answered. Bill knew that Mr. Jones would be in good hands with Virginia.

While he stood at the nurses' station documenting the record of this young man, a highway patrol officer walked into the department and approached him.

"Dr. Blanchard," he began. "I guess you know what happened out there this morning."

Bill recognized the officer, Tim Reed, and was relieved he was the one working the accident. He knew Tim from many other tough encounters such as this, and always found him professional and thoughtful.

"Yeah, Tim. EMS told me about it. But I'd like to hear it from you too. What happened?"

Tim recited the same bleak story given to Bill by the paramedic. He did add that the trucker had sped away but had been stopped several miles down the road. He had been charged with driving with an expired DOT card. Other charges would be pending.

"Thanks, Tim," Bill told him. "That's what I need to know. I guess I'll go back and talk with Mr. Jones." Without thinking, he picked up the clipboard of the young man waiting in the family room.

"Sorry about that, Dr. Blanchard. You know it's against our policy to inform relatives about deceased loved ones. Wish you didn't have to do this."

"I wish no one had to do this. Thanks."

He walked toward the family room, trying to compose a few words that would somehow lessen the pain for this young man, and for himself. Nothing came to mind. It never did.

The family room was located in the back of the department. It was small, ten by ten, containing a small sofa, two chairs, a table and lamp, and a telephone. The bare essentials.

Bill opened the door and found Virginia and Mr. Jones sitting in the chairs. They both looked up as he entered, and they got to their feet. Virginia stepped around Bill and into the doorway.

"I'll be at the nurses' station if you need me," she told him.

From the distraught but puzzled look on Mr. Jones's face, Bill figured that Virginia had not told him anything about his wife's condition. He heard the door close behind him and the two were alone.

He also figured that Mr. Jones knew something terrible had happened and that Dr. Blanchard would not have anything good to tell him.

"Have a seat, Mr. Jones," Bill said, motioning with the clipboard to one of the chairs.

"No thanks, I'll just stand," he responded. "What can you tell me about my wife? How is she? When can I see her?"

He was a large, athletically built young man, six-one or six-two, and he must have weighed two hundred and fifty, easily outweighing Bill Blanchard by more than seventy-five pounds.

Bill was still struggling with how to begin the conversation and how to convey the awful news. Should he be direct, blunt, to the point? Should he gradually ease into the fact that this man's wife was dead, killed instantly in the wreck?

He was turning these thoughts over in his mind as he stepped farther into the room and sat down in one of the chairs. As he did so, he forgot that he was positioning himself dangerously far from the door. Rule Number One: In such a situation, always—always—stand between the family member and the door.

Mr. Jones, in his nervous, purposeless pacing, happened to end up directly in front of the doorway, blocking any rapid exit. Unfortunately, this new circumstance was completely lost on Bill. Momentarily oblivious to the situation, he began what he thought would be the gentlest way to let Mr. Jones know about his wife.

He began by describing the accident, of which the young man had little memory. He explained about the truck driver and his careless high-speed maneuvering. Then he told him about his wife.

"The truck apparently caused you to swerve to avoid a collision, and you lost control of your vehicle. The car flipped several times and your wife was thrown out." He purposefully didn't mention that Mr. Jones had been seat-belted and his wife had not. There would be enough time for self-recrimination in the months and years ahead.

"I'm afraid that when she fell out of the car, she struck her head on the ground. With the speed of the vehicle and the force of the impact, she suffered a significant head injury. I'm sorry I have to tell you this…but she didn't make it. She's gone. But it's certain—"

He was about to tell him she hadn't suffered, that her death had been immediate, but he didn't have the chance. It was then he realized his mistake. The young man in front of him was about to explode, and Bill was in the worst possible position.

Mr. Jones was looking at the floor, trembling, with clenched fists. Bill slowly stood up from his chair, hoping to correct his unthinking mistake.

Too late. Mr. Jones erupted. He grabbed Bill by the throat and effortlessly slung him through the air, then turned and slammed him into the door.

"You son of a b———!" he screamed. "You killed her! You killed my wife!"

There was little Bill could do. He struggled to free himself, but his assailant was too big and too strong. The clipboard fell and clattered on the tiled floor as Mr. Jones repeatedly slammed Bill against the door. And then he began to punch him in the face with a fierceness born of his frustration and grief.

Virginia heard the commotion and immediately ran to help. She tried to open the family-room door. There was no lock on it, but Dr. Blanchard's body was jamming it shut. She pushed as hard as she could but to no avail. She ran back to the nurses' station and called Security.

Two officers arrived within minutes and as they approached, there was an ominous quiet within the room. The door now opened without resistance. They saw Mr. Jones standing in the corner, his back to the door. His head was hanging down and his forehead was pressed against the wall. He was breathing heavily, but he was calm.

Lying motionless on the floor was the body of Bill Blanchard. Blood was dripping from his mouth and there was a small, dark-red pool forming on the cold tile under his face. His glasses were lying beside his head, the lenses shattered and the frames mangled.

He would survive, though it would be weeks before he would be able to return to work in the ER. Three missing teeth, a fractured jaw and eye socket, two broken ribs.

Rule Number One...

❧

7:45 a.m. It was raining. A tropical storm had dealt the coast a glancing blow and we were receiving the remnants of its flanking layers of clouds and the moisture that came with them. The streets were slick, and the visibility was poor.

"We're going to be busy this morning," Amy Conners pronounced to no one in particular. She was straightening out the disorganized paperwork of a busy night, left by her third-shift counterpart. "Always is when it rains like this. You'd think people would learn to drive in bad weather. Slow down, or somethin'. Or stay at home."

She would be right, of course. This rain would result in a lot of fender benders, and potentially a few serious accidents. We would probably see them all.

As if on cue, the EMS radio pierced the fragile calm of our early morning.

"ER, this is Medic 2."

Lori had been checking the medication log. She put the leather-bound notebook on the counter and walked over to the radio.

Picking up the phone she responded. "Medic 2, this is the ER. Go ahead."

"ER, we've got an eighty-two-year-old lady here, auto accident. Full cardiac arrest. She's intubated, no response to any medications. CPR in progress. Should be there in five. Any further orders?"

Lori looked over to me for a response. I shook my head.

"No, Medic 2. Continue CPR. Trauma room on arrival."

"10-4." The radio fell silent.

Lori and I walked across the hallway to the trauma room to make the usual preparations.

"See, I told ya," Amy intoned prophetically. "I'll call the lab and X-ray."

"Thanks," I said. This didn't sound too promising. The chances of survival for this unfortunate woman were very small. Her age, the lack of response to rescue efforts, and the probability this trauma had come from an auto accident all portended a fatal outcome.

It turned out the circumstances surrounding this elderly patient were not what we had assumed. She had been driving her husband to see his cardiologist for his monthly visit. He had a heart attack six months earlier and was doing well. She was enjoying good health and had no significant medical problems. They lived out in the country, on a farm that had been in their family for several generations.

They had been driving into town this morning and she had started to rub her chest. Then she complained of indigestion, which she put down to a hastily prepared and consumed breakfast. Her husband didn't think much of it until he noticed the car was beginning to veer a little toward the curb. He had glanced over at his wife and saw that her head was lolling from side to side. Before he could say or do anything, she had slumped over the steering wheel. The car had swerved completely off the road, slowing and gently coming to rest against a street lamp.

A witness had called EMS, and within a few minutes we had received our call from Medic 2.

She had apparently suffered a massive heart attack and was flat-line when she arrived in the ER. Despite our efforts, there was nothing we could do to change that. She was pronounced dead twenty minutes later.

"Mr. Reid is in the family room, Dr. Lesslie," Lori informed me. "He's there by himself, but I think some family members have been called."

I was finishing my notes on his wife's chart. "Thanks, Lori. I'll be one more minute."

She didn't move, but remained standing by my side. "Do you want me to go back there with you?" she asked.

"No. Thanks, but I'll be okay. Just send his family back when they get here."

I had Mrs. Reid's clipboard in my hand as I stepped into the small family room. Mr. Reid was sitting on the sofa, his hands folded, his gaze fixed on the floor. He was a tall man, of medium build, with a face and neck wrinkled and weathered by many decades in the sun. He looked up as I entered.

Fleetingly, the thought occurred that I needed to position myself between this man and the door. It was a protective reflex, Bill Blanchard's lesson having been indelibly etched into my memory. But this was an eighty-year-old man, hardly a threat.

I stepped across the small space and sat down beside him on the sofa. I shook his hand, and he somehow managed a faint attempt at a smile.

"Mr. Reid," I began. "I need to tell you about your wife."

He nodded slightly, his eyes telling me he already knew what I was going to say. He had known from the moment he had seen her slump over in the car.

We talked for several minutes and then fell silent. He had sobbed for a moment, and then collected himself. He was calm and somehow at peace.

His eyes glistened as he said, "You know, she's had a good life. A good family. Grandchildren that love her. But it hasn't always been easy, workin' a farm all these years. But that's what she wanted. Wouldn't ever consider leavin'."

And then he expressed his concern for his sons and grandchildren. "They're really gonna miss her. They're farmers too, and live on the family land. They see her every day. I don't know what to—"

His last thought was interrupted by the opening of the door. I looked up to see two middle-aged men and a teenage boy stepping into the room. These were big guys. And they all wore well-used, dirt-stained overalls, the badge of men who made their living with their hands. The door closed and the older men sat down in the two chairs. The teenager stood against the door. Their eyes were fixed on Mr. Reid, and then they moved to me.

Bill Blanchard. Suddenly his swollen and bruised face flashed across my mind. I gripped the clipboard in my hands, flimsy protection should I need it.

I was about to say something when Mr. Reid spoke.

"Boys, I hate to tell you this, but Mama's gone." It was a simple statement, but all that needed to be said.

The two men immediately got up from their chairs, and the boy straightened up, bolt-upright in front of the door. Their gaze went from Mr. Reid to me, and back to Mr. Reid.

"Daddy," one of the sons uttered. The single word contained volumes of grief and loss and love. And then they began coming across the room.

Mr. Reid was slowly getting to his feet, seeming much older and weaker than he had a few moments earlier. He seemed unsteady now. I also stood up, and glanced in the direction of the door. The teenager stood motionless, his arms dangling by his side as he stared intently at his grandfather.

One of the men reached out and brushed my shoulder as he

hurriedly stepped forward. In an instant, the two sons held their father in their arms, sobbing.

I stood watching, and it was only then I realized how tightly I had been gripping the clipboard in my hands. I felt small and out of place.

One of Mr. Reid's sons turned to me and said, "Doc, I know one of the paramedics that brought Mama in. I saw him in the parking lot a minute ago and he told me she was in bad shape when they picked her up. He told me you had done everything you could to try and save her. Moss and I here want to thank you for that," he said, motioning with his head to his brother.

He held out his hand to me and I shook it, not knowing what to say.

I stepped out into the hallway and closed the door behind me. I was alone, and I stood there for a few minutes. I looked down at the clipboard in my hand and felt a little foolish. What good would this flimsy piece of glued-together material have done me had these two big men and the teenager turned violent? And then I felt small again, remembering their response to the news of their mother and grandmother. These men, this family, were firmly grounded, and though their loss was sudden and awful, they had somehow maintained their composure. They had supported each other with a tangible love and a quiet dignity.

Yet you never know. You can never really predict how people will respond in these circumstances. You have to be watchful.

Always remember Rule Number One.

I walked back down the hall to the nurses' station.

6

The **Generations Pass**

All men are like grass, and all their glory
is like the flowers of the field.

—Isaiah 40:6

It was a Saturday night around 9:30, and we had been really busy. Most of our rooms were full and the stack of charts for unseen patients kept getting higher.

I picked up the chart from the top of the pile, noted the room location, and headed off in that direction. I glanced briefly at the information at the top of the clipboard:

Minor trauma—C
William Purvis
35 yr old WM
Laceration of chest

"That's a pretty bad one," the triage nurse commented, nodding at the chart in my hand as she passed by.

Great. A complex laceration could take a while to repair, and all during that time the ER would be backing up. Well, we'd just have to see what it looked like.

William Purvis was lying on the stretcher of bed C. It was in the back right corner of minor trauma. Each bed in this room was encircled by ceiling-mounted curtains that could be drawn aside to create more open space or pulled around for privacy. Since he was alone in the room, the curtains had been pulled back and the room was open.

I walked over to his stretcher and pulled out the curtain that separated his bed from the one beside him. Should someone else come into minor trauma, I presumed Mr. Purvis would want some privacy.

"Mr. Purvis, I'm Dr. Lesslie," I announced. "What happened to you this evening?"

He was lying comfortably, propped up by a pillow, and was holding a large gauze bandage across his chest. Blood had oozed through the cotton mesh in a few places.

"This!" he said, removing the gauze and revealing a twelve-inch gash that extended from his left nipple to the pit of his stomach. It was clearly down to muscle, but at the moment there was no bleeding. The pressure he had applied must have helped. He was obviously exasperated, and he dropped the bandage back on his chest.

It was then I noticed he was wearing black leotards and bright-red wrestling shoes. I studied his face for a moment, trying to place his name. He looked familiar, and then...it dawned on me.

"You're one of the Bruiser Brothers, aren't you?" I asked him.

He nodded without looking up at me. "Yeah, I'm Max."

The Bruiser Brothers, Max and Irv, were two of my kids' favorite wrestlers. They were some of the leading "bad guys," and for some inexplicable reason my children identified with them. Hmm. In fact, I had seen them only a few weeks ago when they had come to town. I had been the "event physician" for a big wrestling extravaganza, performing a couple of required licensing examinations before the show. I was then required to be on hand lest something go wrong. It seldom did. These were well-trained athletes and usually things were well-planned and well-choreographed.

"Max, or William, I'm a big fan of yours." I lied a little here. "Tell me more about what happened tonight."

This half of the Bruiser Brothers was enormous. He must have been at least six-foot-five, and the chart said he weighed in excess of three hundred pounds. From what I could see, most of that weight was muscle.

He shifted slightly on the stretcher, wincing from the pain.

"We were wrestling over at the Civic Center this evening," he began. "We'd just finished our bout and I was climbing out of the ring ahead of Irv. Just got down the steps when this old coot sitting on the front row jumps up with a knife and slices me. I got a glimpse of the blade—looked like a big hawkbill—but everything seemed to happen in slow motion. I couldn't get out of the way quick enough—and then this," he pointed to his chest again. "Irv jumped down the steps and coldcocked the guy."

"Wow!" I remarked. "You'd think they'd have better security."

"You'd think," he agreed. "But this guy must have been in his seventies. I'd be more worried about some of the ladies sitting around him. They really get wound up."

"What happened then?" I asked.

"I got out of there as fast as I could, that's what happened," he exclaimed. "That guy was crazy and I wasn't hangin' around. People were screamin' and Irv was yellin' and pushin' me down the aisle. And here I am."

It must have been mayhem. Those wrestling spots were always packed, and the crowd must have really reacted. And I was betting it would be on TV on the coming Saturday.

I had to check myself. Max was a patient now and not a celebrity. I needed to shift back into physician mode. Still, it was kind of interesting having him here. He wasn't a movie star or the vice president, but he was famous, at least in this part of the country. Or maybe infamous.

"Okay, let me take a look at that cut," I said, carefully removing the gauze. As I examined the wound I asked, "Has anything like this ever happened before?"

"You mean gettin' attacked after a bout? No. Not to me. I've never been cut before. Matter of fact, I've never even had stitches. But as far as the wrestlin', no, I've never been hurt. Sure, we get spit on and cussed at. That just goes with the territory. And one time, a lady hit Irv in the head with her pocketbook. But we've never really been hurt."

He paused and shook his head, then glanced down at his exposed chest.

"How bad is it?' he asked.

"Not too bad," I answered. "It'll be fine. You're going to need a few stitches—actually quite a few—but it'll do fine."

Lori came into the room and began setting up a suture tray. I put on my surgical gloves and began the process of anesthetizing the edges of the wound. It took me about forty-five minutes to clean and close the laceration, but it came together nicely and would do well.

During that forty-five minutes, Max and I chatted about the vagaries of being a professional wrestler. It sounded like a difficult lifestyle, certainly not as glamorous as you might imagine. There was a lot of work and a lot of training. And then there was the issue of being a "bad guy." Still, this was fascinating stuff.

As I was putting the finishing touches on my handiwork, I heard Lori come into the room and direct another patient to have a seat on the stretcher beside Max. Her voice came through the drawn cloth curtain.

"Sir," she told the patient, "just make yourself comfortable here and the doctor will be with you as soon as he can."

"Okay," was the muffled reply.

"Looks like you're gonna be busy tonight, Doc," Max whispered, tilting his head in the direction of the adjacent bed.

"Yeah, but it's Saturday night," I answered. "What do you expect? Especially with a bunch of wrestlers in town."

He chuckled, relaxing a little now that we were finished.

"Okay Max, we'll need to take these stitches out in about ten days," I instructed him. "Just keep this clean and dry. I'll give you something for pain in case you need it and some cream to apply a couple times a day. As far as taking out the stitches, you can have your family doctor do it, or if you're in the neighborhood, just come by here."

"Thanks, Doc. Thanks a lot. Maybe I'll see you the next time we come to town," he replied.

"Yeah, maybe so. After I tell my kids about this, I'm sure they'll insist we all go to see you and Irv wrestle. Maybe they'll get to shake your hand."

"That'd be good," he answered. "You just never know."

A nice guy, I thought. Not the scowling, brooding eye-gouger presented on TV.

I stood and stretched, taking my gloves off and tossing them into the trashcan at the foot of the stretcher.

"One of the nurses will be back in just a minute and put a bandage on that," I added in parting.

Stepping toward the door, I glanced at our newest patient. I stopped just out of Max's line of vision and stared. There on the stretcher of bed D sat an elderly man, his hair disheveled and his shirt partially pulled out of his pants. He was looking down at the floor, holding his jaw with both hands. I could see that the left side of his face was swollen and bruised. A small trickle of blood made its way down his chin from the corner of his mouth.

A movement behind me drew my attention from the old man. Max had stood up and was getting his clothes together. He was supposed to wait for the nurse, but he might be getting impatient. I glanced back at this new patient. Was this a bizarre coincidence, or was this Max's assailant? I couldn't take a chance.

Without wasting another second, I stepped into the cubicle of bed D and pulled the curtain on around to completely enclose the area. The old fella looked up at me but didn't say anything. I just stood there and smiled.

Lori walked into the room, asked Max to sit back down, and then dressed his wound.

After a few minutes she said, "There you go, Mr. Purvis, all done. Here's a prescription for something for pain and some directions for taking care of this wound. The stitches come out in ten days. Any questions?"

"No, I think that about does it, ma'am," he said. And then louder, through the curtain, "Thanks again, Doc."

"Sure thing, Max," I answered. The old man kept staring at me, silent and puzzled. I just stood there and continued to smile at him goofily. When I was sure Lori and Max were well out of the room, I relaxed and breathed a sigh of relief.

Whew! I collected myself and then addressed the patient. "I'm Dr. Lesslie. What can we do for you tonight?"

He looked up at me and slowly shook his head. As I looked closely at him, I thought he must be at least eighty. But it was a worn-out eighty, and in his wake were too many cigarettes and too much alcohol.

For a moment he didn't say anything. Maybe he had been drinking and had fallen down, or been in an auto accident and struck his face on the steering wheel.

And then, there it was.

"Doc, I was at the wrasslin' matches tonight." His words came painfully through his injured jaw. "One of them Bruiser Brothers was tusslin' with Jumbo Mullins, and Jumbo was givin' him what for. Then Max, I think it was, started gougin' Jumbo in the eyes and he got him pinned. That ain't fair, especially after the way Jumbo lost his belt to Big Al Gargantua last month. Anyway, I've been pullin' for Jumbo Mullins for about ten years and this just weren't right. Gougin' him in the eyes and all."

He paused here and rubbed his swollen jaw.

"Anyway, I was a hollerin' at the ref, but it didn't do no good. When the bout was over, they came out of the ring and I was just standin' there, mindin' my own business, and one of them boys walked by and punched me! Just outta nowhere! You can ask my nephew, Skeeter. Busted my jaw, looks like."

Funny he didn't mention anything about wielding a hawkbill knife. I knew better than to raise that point.

"Let's take a look there," I said, stepping closer and gingerly examining his bruised and puffy face. There was an obvious step-off in the mandible and I could feel it grinding when he tried to talk.

"I think you're right about your jaw," I told him. "Looks like it's probably broken. But we'll need to get some X-rays to be sure. I'll have one of the nurses bring you an ice pack for that. Just stay put here and we'll get you around to Radiology in a few minutes."

"Dang-nab that boy!" he blurted out. "If he'd a' come straight at me, I think I coulda took him. But no, he had to sucker punch me! Came outta nowhere. That ain't right."

"Well, don't worry about that now." I tried to calm him. "We need to get you taken care of. Just hold on right here."

I pulled the curtain open and stepped toward the doorway.

"That just ain't right!" he muttered again.

I glanced back and caught a glimpse of our would-be pugilist jabbing the air with a clenched fist. The sudden movement jarred his jaw and he flinched, moaned, and again grabbed his face.

I walked up the hall and reflected on what had just transpired. Here was Max Bruiser, a well-known and admired professional wrestler, felled by a wizened, anonymous old fellow, old enough to be his grandfather. I was reminded of a scene from the movie *Patton* as rendered by George C. Scott portraying George W. Patton at the end of his career. The general was telling the story of Roman conquerors who returned triumphantly from battle and proudly rode in their chariot through the city. A slave was instructed to stand behind them and repeatedly whisper a reminder of their fallibility: "All glory is fleeting."

That hasn't lost its meaning.

In further confirmation of this, I realized our elderly brawler's bright and shining moment of glory was quickly coming to an end. Two police officers had just entered the department and were heading toward minor trauma.

⌘

It was 2:00 p.m. on a Wednesday.

"Dr. Lesslie, you might want to go see the guy in room 5," Nancy remarked as we passed in the hallway. She had recently transferred to the department from the pediatric floor and was in triage today. She seemed to be a little perplexed.

Stopping, I looked at her and asked, "What's the problem?"

She turned and faced me, shaking her head. "It's an old man with chest pain. And boy, is he cantankerous. Had some left-sided chest pain for a couple of days and is just now getting it checked out. Blood pressure and pulse are okay, but he wouldn't let me check his temperature. Said he had fever and he knew it and I could just write that down."

"Did you check it anyway?" I asked, assuming that she had not given in to this patient's request. Obtaining accurate vital signs on each patient was important, in addition to being our policy. Once you clearly explained this, most people usually settled down and let you do your work.

"Nope, I didn't. And when you meet this guy, you'll understand why." She turned and walked to the back of the department. "I'm taking a break," she called over her shoulder.

When I reached the nurses' station, the clipboard of room 5 was on the top of the stack of patients to be seen. Curious, I picked it up.

> 89-year-old M with chest pain.
> BP 148/82. Pulse 92.
> Respirations 24.
> Temp ?

I was glancing over to the closed curtain of room 5 when Virginia Granger walked up.

"Know who that is?" she asked, nodding her head in the direction I was looking.

"The man in room 5?" I responded, looking once again at the clipboard.

John Abernathy. The name was familiar, but I couldn't quite place him. His address didn't help. He lived on a street in one of the older, nice neighborhoods in the middle of town.

"That's Dr. Abernathy," she explained. "I watched him come in with Nancy. Hasn't changed a bit since I last saw him. Ten years ago, maybe."

Dr. Abernathy. Now I remembered. He had been a family physician here for forty-some years and had retired a few months before my wife and I had moved to town. That was almost nineteen years ago. Shortly after that, we had crossed paths several times at social functions, and then nothing. Like Virginia, I probably hadn't seen him in ten years, maybe fifteen. And I hadn't heard much of anything about him. Every once in a while someone would tell me that Dr. Abernathy used to be their family doctor. But those people were fewer and farther between all the time.

"Did you ever know him?" Virginia asked me.

"Not really," I answered. "He had retired before I came to the ER. I've met him a few times, but I don't really know him."

"Well, you're in for a treat," she said, grinning. I didn't like the look or sound of that.

"What do you mean, 'a treat'?" I questioned.

"Let's just say that John Abernathy is set in his ways, and can be kind of ornery. Or at least he used to be. Maybe he's mellowed these past few years. But I doubt it. Why don't you go on over there and find out," she prodded, again tilting her head in the direction of room 5.

From what Nancy had said, the chances he had mellowed were slim.

"Hmm," I sighed. "I guess I'll just do that."

I picked up the clipboard and was turning in that direction when Virginia added, "Oh, and I think I remember hearing his wife died about two years ago. Don't think he has any family in the area, so he might be all alone. Thought you might need to know that."

"Thanks, Virginia," I told her. "That might be helpful."

Pulling aside the curtain of his room, I found Dr. John Abernathy sitting bolt upright on the stretcher. His arms were folded across his chest and there was an unpleasant scowl on his face.

"Do I know you?" he asked, more accusing than questioning.

I pulled the curtain closed behind me and sat down on the stool beside his gurney.

"Dr. Abernathy, I'm Dr. Lesslie," I said, introducing myself. "I think we've met a few times in the past."

He studied my face. "Hmm, you do look a little familiar," he conceded, a little less harsh now. "You work here in the ER?"

John Abernathy appeared younger than his eighty-nine years. He still had a full head of wavy gray hair, and his eyes were clear, blue, and piercing. He was a slender man and appeared fit. He had donned a hospital gown but had kept his T-shirt on, making a quiet but unambiguous statement of defiance and autonomy.

"Yes, I'm an ER physician here at the hospital. This is where I work," I explained.

"Don't have a private practice in town?" he pursued. It occurred to me that John might not be familiar with the practice of emergency medicine and with the staffing of emergency departments with full-time physicians. It had been twenty years since he had been in practice, and things were different now.

"No, I don't have a practice in town. This is where I hang out. After medical school I trained in emergency medicine. It's a specialty now, just like family practice or surgery. You were a family doctor, weren't you?" I asked him, becoming more comfortable now that we seemed to be finding some common ground.

"Yeah, yeah," he answered, stroking his chin and staring up at the ceiling light. "I was a family doctor for forty-three years." Then he looked straight at me again. "Worked right here in this hospital, ya know. Delivered babies, had patients in the ICU with heart attacks, strokes, all of that. Changed some since then," he added, glancing around the room. "Probably couldn't find my way to the cafeteria, much less the ICU."

I began to remember more about John Abernathy, or at least what I had heard about him from other physicians and friends in town. He had been one of the first GPs in the area and had developed the largest practice in the county. By all accounts he was a good physician and people trusted him. They didn't necessarily like him, though. He had a reputation of being blunt and unyielding. And he made it clear that he was the physician and the one in charge. There apparently was little negotiation when it came to treatment decisions or alternatives.

Outside of his office and the hospital, he was still "the doctor." That was his accepted and expected persona. Should some unsuspecting waitress or clerk address him as "Mr. Abernathy," he was quick to inform them he was a physician. "That would be Dr. Abernathy, young man."

"Yeah, come to think of it, I've heard something about you ER doctors. TV show, or something. Tell you what, though. When I was in practice, we took care of our own. Didn't have a doctor spending all of his time in the emergency room. If someone came to the hospital, the nurse in the ER would call us, and if it was something she could handle, she'd just send 'em home or to the office. Something more serious, we'd just stop what we were doing and come on in. Didn't matter whether it was day or night."

He paused, nodding. Then he added, "Yep, we took care of our own."

I thought better of informing him that we were now seeing more than 150 people a day in the ER, as opposed to the 10 or 12 per day who had come through twenty-five years ago. Things *had* changed.

"You know," he went on, "one of the medical wings upstairs is named after me." He studied my face for an acknowledging response.

I struggled momentarily and then suddenly remembered.

Nodding my head and smiling, I said, "Yes, the Abernathy Wing. It's up on the fourth floor. It's a postsurgical area now, but it's still the Abernathy Wing."

A look of satisfaction appeared on his face and he said, "Yep. Named after me. Been a while since I've been up there."

That was a good thing. Though I was glad I had been able to retrieve this information from my remote memory banks, he didn't need to see the plaque bearing his name. It was scratched, tarnished, and mostly hidden by a plastic plant placed in front of it. Its existence had stuck in my mind because of my curiosity about its origin. Now I knew.

"Yep, the Abernathy Wing," he repeated.

Standing up, I placed his clipboard on the counter behind me and asked, "Dr. Abernathy, tell me about this chest pain you've been having."

He looked up and pointed to the left side of his chest, about a handbreadth below his armpit. "Hurts right here when I take a deep breath or lie down. I've had some cough for a couple of days and now a fever. Don't know how high, but I'd guess about 102. I think it's probably pneumonia."

That would be my hunch as well.

"We'll need to get an accurate temperature here, don't you think?" I asked, as benignly as possible.

He looked askance at me and then nodded his head. "I suppose so," he conceded.

Lori had pulled the room curtain aside and stuck her head through the opening. "Everything okay here?" she asked, looking at me. "Do you need anything, Mr. Abernathy?"

He rolled his eyes and was about to speak. I cut him off with, "Lori, we're fine. But would you tell the secretary we'll need some blood work, blood cultures, and a chest X-ray? Thanks."

She left the room. "Does sound like pneumonia, doesn't it?" I remarked. "We'll see what your chest X-ray looks like and if it is, you need to plan on staying in the hospital."

"Thought I might," he answered, frowning and gesturing to a small overnight bag on the floor. "Brought a few things with me, just in case."

Twenty minutes later, we had our answer. Dr. John Abernathy's chest X-ray was hanging on the view box just outside the observation room. He had a large pneumonia in his left lung, explaining the fever, the cough, and the chest pain. At his age this was a serious problem, but with antibiotics and fluids he should be better in a few days.

Virginia Granger walked over and stood beside me. "Pneumonia?" she asked, pointing to the irregular whited-out area in his left chest.

"Yeah, and a pretty good one," I answered.

She looked at me over the top of her bifocals. "I guess you found out he's an interesting bird," she said. "He's been through a lot, I understand. I have a friend who lives on the same street and she tells me that after his wife died a few years ago, he mainly stays in the house. Doesn't get out much at all. And no family here in town." She paused and then, "Pretty lonely, I suppose. And if he has to be admitted to the hospital, he's not going to like it."

Not many people liked the idea of having to go into a hospital, but I was curious about her comment. "Why do you say that?"

"Well, Dr. Lesslie, you may think I'm 'old school,'" she said while adjusting the starched nursing cap seated squarely on the top of her head, "but John Abernathy is *really* 'old school.' He comes from an era when the family doctor was one of the pillars of the community. Everybody knew him and respected him. He couldn't go anywhere without people coming up and shaking his hand and saying they'd never forget how he'd helped their mother, or wife, or son. That's just the way it was. And now…" she sighed, shaking her head. "Well, now…you didn't even recognize him, did you?"

"No, I—"

"And that's okay," she interrupted. "He's been out of the mainstream for a lot of years. I was thinking a minute ago that I'm the only one here in the department who knows who he is. Maybe one of only a handful in the whole hospital. Sorta sad, don't you think?"

It was a rhetorical question, and I waited as she mused. Then she continued, "Sad because he built his whole life around that idea, of his being the town doctor. And now, what does all that matter? Who cares anymore, except maybe him? He's just kind of lost out there, drifting."

She was right, of course. Treating John's pneumonia would be the most straightforward part of his care.

I needed to inform Dr. Abernathy of his diagnosis and that we would be admitting him to the hospital. I was just stepping into room 5 when I overhead Frank, one of our lab techs. "Okay, buddy, this might stick just a little." He was preparing to draw blood from

Dr. Abernathy's left arm. John had winced when Frank said this, but it was not from the anticipated poke of the needle. It was from being addressed as "buddy." That had stung, and I wasn't sure how he was going to respond.

To my surprise, the wince faded to a look of resignation, and he remained silent. His shoulders slumped, and for the first time, he looked like an old man.

My next shift was two days later. Mid-morning, I had the chance to go upstairs and check on some of the patients we had admitted when I had last worked. I especially wanted to check on John Abernathy.

"302," the unit secretary told me. "You'll be his first visitor."

Room 302 was near the nursing station and I only had a short walk. Pushing the door open, I tapped on it lightly. "Dr. Abernathy?"

Hearing no response, I stepped into the room. John was sitting in bed, reclining at 45 degrees, with his head supported by a pillow. The wall-mounted television had not been turned on, and he was staring out the window.

He turned as I entered. "Hello, Dr. Lesslie," he said. "Came by to make sure I hadn't gone AWOL?"

"Yes, as a matter of fact," I responded, smiling. "And to see if you needed anything."

"Well, thanks," he said. "Actually, I think I'm doing pretty well. No more fever and the chest pain is much better. That young whippersnapper of an internist tells me I might be able to go home in a day or two. Still wet behind the ears, but he seems to know what he's doing," he conceded.

"But the food here is terrible," he continued. "Used to be better. Or at least I think it did." He paused then, a perplexed look on his face. "But you know, maybe it's always been terrible. How would I know? I've never been a patient before this."

We talked for a few minutes and then it was time for me to head back to the department.

"Dr. Abernathy, take care of yourself and get better," I told him. "You're in good hands, so just do what they ask you to do, okay?"

"You must have been talking to Virginia Granger," he replied sardonically. "Always had to keep an eye on that one."

I laughed. "Yeah, Virginia has told me a thing or two about you. And yes, you do have to keep an eye on her."

I was pulling the door open to leave when John Abernathy spoke quietly behind me. "Dr. Lesslie...Robert. If you get the chance tomorrow, and I'm still here...would you come by again and we'll chat? But only if you get the chance."

"I'll make the chance, John. If you're still here and not at home," I told him.

"Thanks."

The door closed behind me, and I stood in the hallway for a moment, thinking.

"Excuse us," an orderly spoke from behind me. "Comin' through."

He was pushing a wheelchair occupied by a teenager. The boy was dressed in his street clothes and was probably being discharged. As they rolled by, the door across the hall opened. Two nurses walked out of the room, looked over at me, nodded, and continued their conversation.

"I can't believe she can get away with that," one of the nurses said. Then their conversation faded and became unintelligible as they walked off toward the nursing station.

The overhead intercom crackled. "Dr. Smith, report to Radiology *stat*. Dr. Smith to Radiology."

On it went—life, time, people. For another minute I just watched and listened.

Demon Rum

*Wine is a mocker and beer a brawler; who-
ever is led astray by them is not wise.*

—Proverbs 20:1

U nder the influence of alcohol, people do and say things they
would never dream of when sober. We see this demonstrated
every day in the ER. Sadly, these actions cannot be undone, nor can
these words ever be unsaid. Wine is indeed a mocker.

❦

The voices behind the curtain of room 2 had been quiet enough at
the beginning. The mother and father of our fifteen-year-old patient
had arrived in the department and had just entered the cubicle. They
were checking on their son, asking how he was, making sure he was
okay.

EMS had brought Johnny to the ER after he had been involved in
a minor auto accident. He had recently received his learner's permit,
and it seems he and a couple of friends had clandestinely taken one
of the family cars out for a spin. One of the older boys had managed
to procure two six-packs of beer, and off they went.

It was three o'clock on a warm May afternoon, and it wasn't long
before the beer was consumed. The group decided to tour several
neighborhoods near Johnny's home, with him woozily at the wheel.
He failed to negotiate a sharp turn in Forest Hills Estates and went
on to carve a new driveway through an azalea bed. Then he smashed

a large, concrete birdbath before finally wedging the sedan between two pine trees.

Johnny had banged his forehead on the steering wheel. It was nothing serious, just a few bruises and a small laceration that would need to be repaired. When he tried to exit the car, he found the driver's door firmly jammed by one of the trees. Looking around, he realized his friends were nowhere to be found. They had managed to climb through one of the back windows and had taken off.

Through the fog of his five beers, the young man was beginning to understand his plight. He shuddered as he looked up through the shattered windshield of his father's car. There, on the front steps, stood the lady of the house. She was in her mid-sixties, wearing a floral housedress and a navy-blue apron. She stood stone still, staring at the wreckage of her yard, her fists angrily planted on her hips.

Johnny just shook his head, slumped in the seat, and waited. Within minutes, the police and EMS had arrived.

The voices behind the curtain were becoming a little louder, a little more agitated. It seemed to mainly be the father, but occasionally we could hear the son as well.

"What...! Who were...No, you just hold on...!" A few words and phrases carried across the department. Outbursts and unintelligible pieces of sentences, but clearly the temperature in room 2 was rising.

Amy Conners looked up from her logbook. "You might need to go check on things in there," she said to me, tilting her head in the direction of the voices. "Think I should call Security?"

"No, we won't need that," I assured her. "They'll calm down in a minute. But I'll go over and have a few words with them."

I was reasonably confident in my assessment of the situation. I had briefly spoken to Johnny's parents when they arrived in the ER. They seemed calm enough, though obviously concerned. His father was a professional of some description and was dressed in a business suit. His mother was tall, slender, and very quiet, letting her husband ask the questions for the two of them.

As I made my way to room 2, the sounds coming from behind the curtain took an ominous turn. The distance was only a matter of a few steps. But in the moments it took to cross that brief space, I clearly heard the father yelling at Johnny and Johnny responding with slurred expletives. Then came the sounds of scuffling, of the stretcher being pushed against the wall, and the grunts of two men struggling with each other. Then a woman's scream. And silence.

"Hold on here!" I demanded, pulling the curtain aside and stepping into the room.

I will never forget the bizarre and troubling scene played out before me. Johnny's father stood nearest me, his fists clenched by his side, his hair tousled and his tie flipped over his shoulder. He stood glaring at his son. Johnny was standing only a foot or so from his father. His head was hanging down, and his T-shirt was rumpled and pulled out of his jeans. A thread of blood trickled down his forehead from the still-open laceration. His arms hung limply by his side and he stared at the floor. He swayed a little from side to side, still quite drunk.

Then I noticed his mother. She stood cowering in the back corner of the room, pressing herself against the end of the stretcher and the countertop. She held her face with both hands, her eyes staring. She was looking from her son to her husband, and back to her son again. Tears streamed down her cheeks. The only sound in the room was her muffled sobbing.

Her jaw had been shattered by Johnny's punch.

An operation would repair the fractured bone, but that blow could never be taken back. It would be a part of this family, of this relationship, forever.

Later, at the nurses' station, I looked up from the clipboard of room 2 and put down my pen. I stared at the closed curtain across from me. I had just remembered something. Next Sunday would be Mother's Day.

It was 10:30 on a Friday evening. Sometime between six o'clock and midnight usually marks the official beginning of the weekend. Our volume will pick up, and the nature of our patient encounters begins to change. It's not a coincidence that this time of the week marks the beginning of an increase in alcohol consumption. More wrecks, more falls, more fistfights. Everybody seems to be having a big time.

This particular overnight shift had thus far proven to be typical. We had already had a knifing and a moped accident. The knifing was a superficial laceration of a young man's buttocks, inflicted as he attempted to escape the grasp of an acquaintance he had just whacked over the head with a beer bottle. The moped accident was more interesting. Three large individuals had attempted to ride this small conveyance at the same time, convinced they would be able to jump a low rock wall on the edge of a field. Gravity had reared its ugly head, and I would have a few of theirs to suture. Nothing serious.

Jeff and I were standing at the nurses' station talking about this daredevil trio, when the automatic ambulance doors hissed open, announcing the arrival of new business. We both looked up to see one of our EMS units wheeling two stretchers into the department.

Denton Roberts was guiding the first gurney into the ER, and he stopped adjacent to where we stood. On the stretcher was a thirty-year-old woman, awake and looking around. Her face was pale, her expression anxious, and there were a number of abrasions on her forehead. Pieces of glass were scattered through her long blonde hair.

"What happened here?" I asked Denton, reflexively taking her wrist and checking her pulse. It was a little fast, but strong and regular. An IV had been inserted into the back of her other hand and was connected to a bag of saline that hung from a pole at the head of the stretcher. I could see it was flowing wide open.

"Auto accident out on Highway 5," he answered. He nodded behind him at the following stretcher. "The guy there was driving. Both of them have had a little too much to drink. Actually, he's pretty soused and he went off the road, into a ditch. She's complaining of belly pain and he has some back pain. Both of their vital signs are okay.

No loss of consciousness. She was still seat-belted in the car. When we got there, he was walking around in the middle of the road. Put 'em both in full spinal protocol and started IVs. He looks all right, but you're gonna have fun," he finished, with a wry smile.

"What do you mean?" I looked in the direction of our second victim.

"Well, let's just say he's not a happy camper," Denton added, nodding.

If I had any doubt as to his meaning, I was quickly enlightened. "Full spinal protocol" meant that a person would be strapped down on a rigid backboard, arms by their sides, legs straight out, and head and neck strapped in place, allowing no movement. This was necessary to protect someone with obvious or potential spinal injuries. But it was also very uncomfortable.

"Get me off this thing!"

Sandy Green, Denton's partner, was struggling with our next guest. Sandy was trying to guide the stretcher into the department with one hand and attempting to keep the patient from falling off with the other.

"And get this thing out of my arm!" He was referring to the IV that had been placed in his right elbow, which he was clumsily attempting to grasp. Sandy needed another hand, maybe two.

"Jimmy, you be still and let them help you." The calm and plaintive admonition came from the young woman in front of me.

"I don' need no help! I need to get outta here!"

Jeff had already moved toward the second stretcher and was trying to help Sandy maintain order.

"Hold on a minute, Jimmy," he instructed him. "Let us just get you to a bed and check you over, and then you can get out of here, okay?"

"I don' need to be checked over! Just lemme get up from here!" was the response.

I looked up at Denton. "Take them back to minor trauma. A and B. I don't think there's anyone in there right now."

"Okay, Doc," he answered, and he started down the hall with his patient.

As Sandy came by the nurses' station, I patted him on the shoulder. He was a large man, and he was sweating profusely. "Just follow Denton," I told him.

He nodded without saying a word.

I glanced down at his patient. He was probably in his early thirties, dressed in blue jeans and a T-shirt, and he had on running shoes. His long jet-black hair looked dyed and was unkempt. On his right forearm was a large tattoo. The name "Amanda" was emblazoned in black ink over a large red heart. Other than this tattoo, I didn't see a mark on him—no scratch, no blood. Nothing.

"Sheryl!" he called out. "Where they takin' you?"

Sheryl? I glanced again at the tattoo. Hmm. Love is a fickle thing.

"Just relax, Jimmy." Sandy tried to calm him. "We're going with her. Just hold on."

They moved off down the hallway, with Jimmy eloquently expressing his displeasure with the current circumstances.

"I told you to get me off this thing!"

While I finished up with two other patients, Jeff made an assessment of our auto accident victims. He walked up to the counter with their charts in his hands.

"Finally got Jimmy calmed down," he told me. "I don't know how long he'll stay that way, though. He's pretty drunk. And pretty obnoxious. He's on bed A. Looks okay, just complainin' of low back pain. But he's movin' around pretty good."

I finished up the chart I was working on and put it into the "Discharge" basket. "Good. And what about her?"

"I don't know. I think she's got somethin' goin' on," Jeff said. "Heart rate's about 110, and her belly is tender. Blood pressure is 110 over 70. Everything else seems okay. I upped her IV."

"Good," I responded. "I'll go take a look."

I had worked with Jeff long enough to know that when he thought something was going on, it usually was. He didn't overreact, and he'd seen a bunch.

Tammy, one of our evening nurse techs, was in minor trauma with our two patients. They were on adjacent beds with a curtain separating them. Jimmy was lying quietly for the moment, his eyes closed. I walked over to bed B.

"How are you feeling, Sheryl?" I asked.

She looked up at me. "Not too good, Doc. What's wrong with me?"

"We're going to find out," I told her, as I gently began to palpate her abdomen. Jeff was right. It was tender and was becoming distended.

"Does this hurt over here?" I asked, pushing down on her left upper belly, just below the rib cage. The spleen lives here, and I was suspicious it might have been injured in the accident. If it was ruptured and bleeding, that might account for the distension.

"Ooh! Yes! That hurts!" she cried out, but still remained calm.

I stopped pressing and took my hands off.

"Okay, we won't do that again," I told her. "But it looks like you might have injured something in your abdomen, maybe your spleen, so we're going to get a CT scan as fast as we can. I'm also going to have one of our surgeons take a look at you."

"Is it bad, Doctor?" she asked.

"Well, it depends on what we find," I answered. "But we'll get it fixed, whatever it is. Okay?"

"Okay," she sighed, and closed her eyes.

Before I turned to leave I asked, "Oh, and one other thing. Have you had anything to drink tonight?"

I could smell alcohol on her breath, but she didn't appear to be intoxicated.

She didn't hesitate with her answer. "Just one beer. That's all."

I made a note on the chart, believing her. The usual response in the ER to this question is "Two beers, Doc." It doesn't matter how smashed a person appears, it's always "two beers." I suppose the honesty switch gets turned off when your blood alcohol reaches a certain level.

Moving to bed A, I made a quick assessment of her partner. He was snoring now, and he barely opened his eyes as I examined him. His vital signs were completely normal and I could find no evidence of any significant injury.

I did manage to rouse him enough to ask a question. "How much have you had to drink tonight, Jimmy?"

"Two beers," was the slurred response. I didn't write that down.

At the nurses' station I asked the unit secretary to see if Tom Daniels was in the hospital. He was the surgeon on call tonight, and if he was around, I wanted to catch him before he went home.

A few minutes later she picked up the phone, then covered the mouthpiece and said, "Dr. Daniels is in the OR, finishing up a case. Do you need to talk with him? It's the OR supervisor."

"No," I told her. "Just ask him to stop by the ER when he's finished. Tell him I might have a spleen for him."

She relayed the message and hung up. "He should be here in about ten minutes," she told me.

They were ready for Sheryl in CT, but ten more minutes wouldn't make much difference. We could wait.

"Jeff, Jimmy in minor trauma will need a urine," I instructed him. "Just check for blood. We'll make sure he didn't injure his kidneys and then he should be able to go."

"Sure," he answered. "But he'll have to use a urinal. I don't think he can walk."

"You're right," I said. "Good luck with that. You may not even be able to wake him up."

Jeff went into the supply room and came out with one of our stainless steel urinals. He walked down the hall toward minor trauma, and I was a few steps behind him.

I was about to turn into the four-bed room when I caught sight of Tom Daniels coming around the corner in the back of the department. He still had on his surgical scrubs and cap.

"Long night?" I asked him.

"Long day," was his response. "It's been nonstop. The OR said you might have something for me. A possible spleen?"

"Yeah, she's right in here."

I led him into minor trauma and noticed Jeff trying to rouse our somnolent patient in bed A. We moved past that bed and behind the curtain separating him from bed B.

"Sheryl, this is Dr. Daniels," I said to her. "He's the surgeon on call tonight, and I wanted him to take a look at you."

Tom walked over to the side of the stretcher. "Sheryl, is it? I'm Tom Daniels. Dr. Lesslie tells me you've been having a pretty rough night."

He proceeded to examine her, asking questions as he proceeded. As he palpated her abdomen she moaned and shifted herself on the bed. He looked up at me and nodded.

"Sheryl, I agree with Dr. Lesslie. Something's going on inside your belly and we're probably going to need to go to the operating room to find out what that is. We'll get the CT scan first, and then decide on a plan. Okay?"

"Okay, Doctor," she answered. "I just want to stop hurting."

As she was saying these last words, I heard some grunting from behind me on the other side of the curtain. I had been aware of some unusual noises behind us, but this was louder and more ominous. Then, "Ooh! Enough!"

Then more grunting and the sounds of a struggle. Suddenly, the urinal flew across the room, clanging loudly against the ceiling light over bed C, then the IV pole in the corner, and finally the floor. It spun around a few times and came to a stop.

Jeff had been trying to get a urine specimen from Jimmy, and Jimmy was not being compliant. When he had first been roused from his alcoholic slumber, he had struck out with a fist, catching Jeff cleanly on the left ear. Then he'd kicked him twice, once in the stomach and once on his thigh. The final straw came when he grabbed Jeff's forearm and drew blood with his fingernails.

Tom Daniels looked at me. I turned, pulling back the curtain.

The grunting was coming from Jimmy, and for good reason. For a moment I watched, mesmerized. Jimmy was still flat on his back on the bed. But Jeff was straddling him, his big left hand pressing down on his chest. Every minute or so, Jimmy would squirm and struggle and try to kick him.

"Aaaaah! Get off me!"

Then he tried to spit into Jeff's face. Jeff was too quick and managed to dodge the liquid projectile. But Jimmy's action led to an unexpected and unwanted result. Jeff's right hand had been poised just above Jimmy's face, and now he quickly thumped him across the bridge of his nose. It was not a forceful blow, not enough to break the skin or any bones. But it was enough to get his attention. It smarted and Jimmy let out a yelp.

"Ooh, get off me!"

The cycle repeated itself. For a few seconds, Jimmy would be still. Then he would start squirming again, trying to kick Jeff. And once again he tried to spit on him. Then a quick pop to the face.

"Ooh! Somebody get him off me!"

It was then I noticed Jeff's eyes. I had seen him angry before, but fortunately not very often. It usually took a lot to provoke him. His face would turn red, he would get very quiet, and then it would blow over. But this time it was different. Jimmy must have found the right buttons tonight. Jeff's eyes were mere slits and his pupils were pinpoints. I shuddered.

Here was one of our best nurses, a hulk of a man. And he was strong. Yet I had seen these huge hands gently hold a two-month-old and deftly start an IV in its tiny hand. And I had watched as he almost tenderly lifted a ninety-year-old woman from her wheelchair onto an examining bed. But I never dared say that to him.

Tonight he was a different person—someone I hadn't expected to see, and someone who scared me a little.

"Doc!" Jimmy had noticed me standing beside the stretcher. "Get him off me!"

Jeff still straddled Jimmy's body, his right hand poised just above his face.

I glanced at Jeff but he was staring intently at his patient.

I looked again at the pleading man on the bed. "Jimmy, if you'll behave yourself, I'll try to get him off you. But you'll have to behave. No more kicking and no more spitting."

"Okay! Okay! Just get him off me!" he replied.

Jeff was not moving. He seemed not to be impressed with Jimmy's sincerity or newfound contrition. I wasn't so sure myself.

"Jimmy, I'll try to do that, but you'll have to promise to calm down. Do you hear me?" I asked him. "No more kicking."

Tom Daniels had walked over and now stood at my shoulder. He surveyed the scene while stroking his chin, an amused look on his face. "Make him cross his heart and pinky swear," he whispered in my ear.

I looked at him and frowned. "Tom, I'm trying to save this man's life," I chided.

"Please, Doc, get him off!" Jimmy was wearing down, and I thought it would be safe to rescue him.

"Jeff, it's time to let him up. Come on, hop off that bed," I tried to persuade him.

Without a word and with an unexpected agility, Jeff sprang to the floor. He walked over to the corner of the room to pick up the urinal, pressing the wrinkles out of his scrubs with the palms of his hands.

Jimmy wasted no time and certainly not this opportunity. He sat up on the bed and dangled his feet over the edge, trying to locate the floor.

"I've had enough! You guys are crazy! I'm outta here!"

"Jimmy, just calm down," I told him. "We'll be glad to check you out, but you're going to have to behave. Just keep your seat."

It was to no avail. Jimmy was determined to get himself out of our department.

"I said I'm outta here and I am!" He got to his feet and with better balance than I had anticipated, he walked to the doorway. He stumbled once and turned in the direction of Jeff. "You're one crazy #$%#&!" And then he was gone.

Tom Daniels looked in Jeff's direction. "Jeff, you okay?" he asked.

"Mm-hmm," was the response. He was okay. He was not back to himself yet, but he was okay. He walked over to bed B. "She need anything else right now?" he asked us, his face still red from his recent activity.

"No," Tom replied. "Just keep her IV going wide open and let's get that CT as fast as we can."

Sheryl had her CT scan: a ruptured spleen and probable torn intestine. Thirty minutes later, she was in the OR and had just been put to sleep.

I was alone, sitting behind the nurses' station. The door to triage opened and an elderly man came into the ER. He walked over to the counter and slapped both hands down in front of him.

"Are you the doctor?" he asked me.

"Yes, I'm Dr. Lesslie," I answered. "What can I do for you?"

"I'm Stanley Wells, Jimmy's daddy," he answered. I sat up a little straighter in my chair. "And I wanted to have a word with you."

I studied him for a moment. I guessed he was fifty-five, maybe sixty years old, though he looked much older. His face was worn and wrinkled and he stood hunched over. Too many hard days and harder nights. And too many years with Jimmy.

"Yes, what about Jimmy?" Several thoughts came to my mind. He had collapsed in the waiting room. He had gone home to get a gun. He was calling the police. But it was none of the above.

"I just want to apologize. I know he's a handful. Obnoxious young buck, especially when he's been drinkin'. And he's pretty drunk tonight," he told me. "I understand he caused quite a ruckus back here."

"Well, he did get a little rowdy, Mr. Wells," I said, taken a little off guard but definitely relieved. "I guess you know he was involved in a pretty serious auto accident?"

"Yeah, I've already talked to the police about it," he answered. "How is that woman, Sheryl? I think he met her at the bingo parlor last week. Seems like a nice girl. She gonna be okay?"

"Well, she's in the operating room right now. She has some internal damage and bleeding, but she's in good hands and I think she'll be alright," I answered.

"Doggone that boy! I told him a hundert times to stop drinkin', and 'specially not to drive when he has been. But he don't listen. Never has, and I guess he never will. Three DUIs, and now this. I don't know what I'm gonna do with him."

He paused and studied the backs of his gnarly hands.

"Anyway, Doc, I just wanted to come back here and apologize for the way my boy acted. I hope he didn't hurt no one."

"No, he didn't. But we were trying to check him over for any injuries when he took off. I think he's going to be okay, but if he wants to be looked at, just bring him back here."

"Thanks, Doc, but I doubt if he wants to come back in here. He's sittin' out in the waiting room with the police and I think he's gonna be leavin' with them. He's in some trouble this time. He ain't got no driver's license, and he's already smarted off to the cops a coupla times."

He paused and shook his head. "I think he's okay though. He ain't complainin' of any pain or anything. But if he changes his mind, I'll bring him straight back."

"You do that, Mr. Wells," I told him. "If you have any questions about Jimmy, just bring him back or give us a call."

He stood straight up now, and put his hands in his pockets.

"Okay, and thanks. But like I said, I'm real sorry for the way he acted out."

"Don't worry," I said. "And I hope you have a better night."

I watched as he walked back out through triage.

Twenty minutes later, Jeff stood with me at the nurses' station. He was at my left elbow and was writing Sheryl's chart, making sure all we had done was duly noted. Moments earlier, Tom Daniels had relayed a message to us through the OR scrub nurse. Sheryl was fine. Her spleen had indeed been ruptured and had needed to be removed. Everything had gone well and he was now closing up. Maybe Sheryl would learn something tonight. Not necessarily about meeting guys at a bingo parlor, but maybe about not riding with someone who had been drinking. It would be a costly lesson.

I heard footsteps behind me, coming from the triage entrance.

"Doc." The voice sounded familiar, but the tone was different. I turned around to see Mr. Wells once again, now standing before me.

"Yes, Mr. Wells. What can I help you with?" I asked him. "Does Jimmy want to be seen now?"

Jeff kept writing on the chart in front of him, never looking up.

"Not exactly, Doc," Mr. Wells announced, a perceptible edge to his voice. "I want to talk with you a minute."

"Sure," I replied. "What's the problem?"

"Well, I just went out and was talkin' with Jimmy. The police have taken him down to the station, but before he left, he told me somethin' that was pretty disturbin'."

"And what was that?" I was afraid I might already know the answer.

"Jimmy told me that when he was back here the doctor jumped on him and beat him up. Held him down and kept hittin' him in the nose."

He paused and stepped closer to me, his face only inches from mine. And he was angry.

"Now I know that Jimmy can get obnoxious when he's been drinkin', but that ain't no call for you to beat up my son, Doc. What with him bein' under the influence and unable to protect hisself and all. That just ain't right and I'm here to complain about it."

He stood with his hands on his hips, indignant.

Jeff never looked up from his work. He just kept writing.

"Mr. Wells, let me say a couple of things," I began. "First of all, I am the only doctor on duty tonight. And secondly, I did not hold your son down and I certainly did not hit him in the nose."

"Well, somebody did!" he exclaimed. "I can see the red marks on his nose, and Jimmy said a doctor done it, and he don't lie to me. Well…not usually."

"Let me say it again, Mr. Wells, and I know you're upset, but I'm the only doctor back here, and I did not beat up your son."

I tried to be as convincing as possible, but he was not yielding.

"Now listen to me, Doc—" he started again.

But I interrupted with, "Mr. Wells, let me tell you what happened back here. We were trying to evaluate your son, to check him out and make sure everything was okay. But he became obnoxious, as you said earlier. And he started cursing and spitting and kicking. And finally, one of the nurses had to sit on him and make him behave."

I peeked at Jeff out of the corner of my eye. He had stopped writing, but he didn't move. He just looked down at the chart on the countertop.

Mr. Wells backed away. He was obviously trying to digest this new information. Then he held his hands outstretched in front of him, palms up.

"You mean to tell me that a nurse beat up my boy?" he asked, incredulous.

"That's right, Mr. Wells," I told him. "A nurse had to make him behave."

Jeff didn't move.

"You mean a nurse…" he muttered, visibly slumping.

"Yes, Mr. Wells, a nurse had to make your son behave," I confirmed.

He stood staring at the floor, silent for a moment.

"A nurse beat up my boy. Well, I'll be doggoned."

He never once looked in Jeff's direction.

Then Mr. Wells straightened himself, held out his hand to me, and said, "Well, Doc, I want to thank you for trying to help my boy. And I apologize again for his behavior. I know ya'll did all you could for him."

I shook his hand. "No problem, Mr. Wells. I hope that everything goes alright for you and your boy."

He nodded, turned, and shuffled toward the triage door.

"I can't believe it," he muttered. "A dang nurse beat up my boy."

He stepped through the door and was gone.

"Quick! Get me a number 4 airway tube!"

We were going to lose the eight-month-old if we couldn't secure his airway.

"And get respiratory down here, *stat!*" I added.

Less then a minute earlier, EMS had burst through the ambulance entrance doors, carrying this young child. "Head injury," Denton, one of the paramedics, had called out, heading straight to major trauma. "Barely breathing and not much of a pulse!"

Lori and I had hurried into the room and quickly assessed the infant. Denton had laid him on the stretcher and then taken a step back. He was breathing hard and was obviously upset. The baby had no muscle tone and only a faint, slow heart rate. There was no immediately obvious injury, but I quickly noticed that his pupils were markedly dilated and deviated to the right. That was not a good sign.

Within minutes, he had been intubated and a respiratory therapist was carefully forcing air into his lungs with an ambu bag. Lori had an IV going and was making sure he was not too chilled. His oxygen saturation had improved with the ventilation of his lungs, as had his heart rate and cardiac output.

With a sigh of relief, I stood up straight and looked around the room for the delivering paramedic. Things were stable for the moment and I needed a better idea of what was going on here.

I located him at the foot of the stretcher and I asked, "Denton, what's this about a head injury? Do you have any idea what happened?"

Denton was making notes on the EMS clipboard. He looked up and said, "We got a call to Jones Avenue, about a child having trouble breathing. When we got there, well, it was absolute chaos. There must have been ten or twelve people in the house and they were all screamin' and hollerin'. Someone said he fell and hit his head. Couldn't get any sense out of any of them. I think they were all drunk. Anyway, his parents were behind us in a truck and should be here any minute."

He stopped and resumed writing up his report. Looking up again he added, "Oh, and Doc, the parents are drunk too."

We would need a CT scan of the child's head, and Lori was going to the nurses' station to get it ordered. As she opened the door, three people bowled their way into the room, pushing her back against the counter.

"Where's my baby? Where's JJ?" This came from one of the two women. Denton was right. She was clearly intoxicated. She staggered as she made her way to the side of the stretcher.

"How is my baby?" she asked, struggling to focus her blurred vision on the small body lying before her. She was barefooted, as were her two companions. Like them, she wore cut-off blue jeans and a dirty T-shirt. "Is he gonna be alright?"

Lori had called for the CT scan from the open doorway and now came back to the stretcher. She was trying to calm these visitors and restore order. I tried to explain the situation in terms they would understand, and tell them what our immediate plans were.

The mother's name was Maylees, and it turned out the other woman, Jenny, was Maylees's sister and JJ's aunt. The man was in his mid-twenties. His name was Bubba, and he was Maylees's common-law husband. We assumed he was also the father of the baby.

Jenny had walked over and wrapped her arms around her sister, though this didn't provide much support. They listed to one side and had to take a quick step to right themselves. Bubba stood back from the stretcher, leaning against the wall. His eyelids were half closed and his head was bobbing. He was also obviously drunk. I wondered who had driven the truck.

"Maylees, can you tell me what happened to your son?" I asked.

She glanced in Bubba's direction and then said, "Yeah, we had some friends over this afternoon, and JJ was in the kitchen and must have tripped and fell and hit his head."

"Yeah, that's right," Jenny slurred in agreement.

I was distracted by a movement in the corner of the room and looked over to Bubba. In spite of his alcohol content, he was really quick. A cigarette was dangling from the corner of his mouth and before I could say anything, he had taken his lighter from his pants pocket and was clicking it. A small flame appeared at the tip of the lighter, and he was leaning forward, his hands cupping the cigarette.

"Hold on there, Bubba," I called out. "You can't smoke that thing in here. Put that lighter out."

Responding to his name, he looked up. "Huh? Oh, okay," he said sluggishly. He extinguished the lighter, took the cigarette out of his mouth, and carefully placed it behind his right ear.

Now, what had Maylees just told me? She had been telling me how JJ had hurt his head.

"He tripped and fell in the kitchen?" I asked, resuming my questioning.

Lori looked over at me, a doubtful expression on her face. Why that look? Wait a minute...JJ was seven-and-a-half months of age, still an infant. Unless he was a prodigy, he probably wasn't walking. This answer didn't make sense. Something else was going on here. I nodded to Lori.

Before I could ask another question, two radiology techs came into the room.

"We're ready for him in CT," one of them reported.

"You can all wait in here if you want," I told the three. "This should not take long, and as soon as we know something, I'll let you know."

Maylees and Jenny backed away from the stretcher, making room for the techs. "You take care of him, now," Maylees told them.

"Yeah, take care of him," Jenny echoed.

Forty minutes later we had our answer. I had walked around to the Radiology Department and was reviewing the child's head scan with the radiologist.

"Here is a skull fracture," he pointed, indicating a starburst pattern on the back of JJ's skull. That indicated a significant and direct blow. "And here's a good bit of blood in his head. See how everything's shifted over?"

The findings were obvious. "Yeah, but that should be able to be drained, don't you think?"

"Should be, but that's not the real problem," he continued. "Look right here."

He pointed to the base of the skull where it sat upon the atlas, the first cervical vertebra. The atlas was displaced a good two and a half centimeters posteriorly. His spinal cord had been severed.

"This kid's dead, or soon will be," he said matter-of-factly.

He was right, of course. There was nothing anyone could do for JJ. I just stood there a few minutes, looking at the films.

As I walked back to the department, I considered my options in dealing with this child's parents. They would need to know the full extent of his injuries and the inevitable outcome. First though, I needed to know what really happened to JJ.

When I reached the nurses' station, I asked Lori to come with me to major trauma. JJ would be following us in a few minutes.

I opened the door, and we found Maylees and Jenny sitting on the stretcher, their legs hanging over the edge. Bubba was sitting on the floor in the corner of the room. His legs were splayed in front of him and his head drooped on his chest.

"How's JJ?" Jenny asked.

"He's about the same," I answered. "And they should be on their way back here with him now. But there's something on his scan that doesn't make sense," I told them.

Maylees and Jenny looked at each other and then at me.

"You told us he tripped and fell in the kitchen," I continued. "But what doesn't make sense is that his head injury is mainly on the back. When kids trip, they usually fall forward."

I paused and studied their faces, waiting for a response. They looked at each other again and then back at me. Bubba just stared at the floor.

"So, tell me. Does JJ really walk? And if he doesn't, then tell us what really happened."

They were silent for a moment and then Jenny spoke up. "No, JJ doesn't walk. And he didn't trip, or anything. Bubba..." she said, nodding at the slumping figure in the corner, "Bubba had him out on the concrete patio and was throwin' him up in the air and catchin' him. JJ was screaming, scared to death. And everyone was laughin'. So Bubba just kept throwin' him up, and then...then...he dropped him. And his head hit the concrete. And he was just layin' there. That's how it happened."

Maylees was nodding her head in agreement.

Lori had closed her eyes upon hearing this. My knees became weak for an instant as I thought of my own children. And then I became angry.

The opening of the door drew my attention, and I watched as Lori walked out toward the nurses' station. She would be calling the police.

Wine is indeed a mocker. And too often a murderer.

8

It **Must** Have Been a **Miracle**

*You are the God who performs miracles; you dis-
play your power among the peoples.*

—Psalm 77:14

Yeah, Doc. I had this spot on my lungs a year or so ago and now
it's gone. A miracle, don't you think?"

A miracle. I have never personally witnessed anything I would call
a miracle of healing, nor have any of my colleagues—at least that they
have told me about. And I have never read of any such occurrence
documented in the medical literature.

This is not to say that wondrous things don't happen every day in
the medical field. I think it's pretty amazing that a broken wrist, if
properly immobilized and left alone, will heal in three or four weeks.
Or that a lacerated forehead, with appropriate attention, will heal itself
in a matter of days. What cardiac surgeons are able to do borders on
the miraculous: stop a beating heart, reroute and restore a compro-
mised blood supply, and start the heart beating again.

But even though I have no personal testimony concerning a verified
miracle of healing, I continue to be impressed by everyday encounters
that come close.

For instance, an impressive clinical encounter is the handling of
a diabetic who has taken too much insulin. Your blood sugar starts
to drop, and at dangerously low levels, you lose consciousness. Most
diabetics recognize the symptoms leading up to this and know to get
some sugar into their systems. A new diabetic, or one who takes poor
care of himself, will come to the ER unconscious or comatose. The

history will usually give us the correct diagnosis. A quickly given load of IV glucose will rapidly resolve this condition. The comatose patient sits up and asks, "What's going on?" It's like turning on a light. Not exactly a miracle, to be certain, but surely something special.

And so, while miracles are not necessary or essential to my faith, I continue to be open to the miraculous. In fact, a few years ago I thought I had happened upon just such a case.

❦

Christmas Eve. I was unlucky enough to have drawn the short straw and was working the night shift. You would think the ER wouldn't be busy on this pre-holiday night. To the contrary, most holidays are among our busiest times. All of the doctor's offices in town are closed, there is usually a liberal amount of alcohol flowing, and people just seem to get lonely.

It was 9:30 p.m. and I was standing at the nurses' station, talking with our ward secretary, Marcella James.

"Any big plans for tomorrow?" I asked her. She was a young woman, early twenties, and I knew she had two small children.

"Nope, gonna be workin' here," she answered. "The hospital's paying a big bonus and I couldn't pass it up. I do get a chance to be home in the morning with the children, though. That'll be good."

The triage nurse placed the chart of a new patient in the "To Be Seen" basket. I turned around and watched as she led a teenage girl and her mother down the hall. She directed the two into our Gyn room and then closed the door behind them.

"Hmm, wonder what that is?" I mused.

"Tonight, could be anything," Marcella opined.

I picked up the new chart and began to read.

> Samantha Towers.
> 15-year-old female.
> Chief complaint: abdominal pain and nausea.

I looked down to her vital signs. Blood pressure and pulse were recorded as normal. No fever. All that was good.

"Well, I guess I'll go find out."

After tapping lightly on the exam room door, I pushed it opened and stepped in.

"Samantha Towers? Hello, I'm Dr. Lesslie," I said, looking at the young girl who was now sitting on the exam table. Her knees were drawn up to her chin, and she had covered herself with a hospital sheet. Her toes were peeking out and I noticed her nails had recently been painted bright red. Closing the door behind me, I addressed the older woman who was sitting on a stool in the corner. "And you're…?" I paused, leaving room for a response.

"I'm Samantha's mother, Sarah Stroud," she stated.

Two different last names. I glanced at the medical chart and quickly noted that the "single" box in the marital status section had been checked.

Ms. Stroud was very perceptive. She had noticed my furtive glance at the clipboard. "I got divorced when Sam—Samantha—was ten. She wanted to keep her last name." She shrugged. "All the same to me."

"Okay, good," I remarked, pulling over the other stool in the room and sitting down. I put the chart in my lap and both hands on my knees. Leaning forward a little, I asked, "Samantha? Would you rather be called Sam, or Samantha?"

"Sam would be fine," she whispered.

"Speak up, Sam," her mother directed. "He's got to be able to hear you."

"Sam is fine," she repeated, louder this time, followed by a sideways glance at her mother.

"Okay, Sam. What's the problem tonight? What brings you to the ER?"

She looked at her mother.

"Go ahead and tell him, Sam," Mrs. Stroud said. "Tell him why we're here."

Sam looked back at me. "It's my stomach," she said. "It's been hurtin'."

"Alright," I coaxed. "And when did this start?"

This was going to take a while. I almost looked down at my wristwatch, but then I remembered Mrs. Stroud. She would probably catch me. I shifted my weight on the stool.

It turned out that Sam had been experiencing some vague lower abdominal pain for about three weeks. It had gotten a little worse over the past few days, but now the main problem was nausea. Every morning she awoke with severe nausea, and by noon she had vomited half a dozen times. There had been no fever, no bleeding, and no trauma. She had no history of any significant medical problems.

Hmm. A young woman with abdominal cramping and morning sickness. This was starting to sound a little familiar.

"Sam, when was your last period?" I asked her.

She immediately looked at her mother.

Sarah Stroud quickly spoke up. "She's never missed a period. Regular as a clock. The last one was…when? Two weeks ago?" she asked her daughter.

"Yeah, that's right," Sam answered, nodding vigorously. "It was two weeks ago today."

"Okay," I responded, placing a question mark in the box entitled "last menstrual period." Something didn't seem right here.

"Now, Sam. I need to ask you a few personal questions." I glanced over at her mother who was staring at me with pursed lips, waiting.

Looking back at Samantha, "Have you ever been sexually active? Ever had sex with anyone?" I asked as delicately as I could.

"Good Lord, no!" her mother answered for her. "This child is a virgin! Why, of course not. You tell him so, Sam."

I had kept my eyes on Sam during this exchange. She had been watching her mother and had not blinked an eye. She remained completely impassive.

She looked at me then and coolly said, "No, Doctor. I have never had sex."

"Are you—" I tried to pursue the issue.

"There. See? She's never had sex," her mother interrupted. "Now, can you please tell us what you think is the matter with Sam? What is causing her pain and vomiting?"

I shifted my feet and studied the medical chart, weighing my options. It appeared obvious that any further direct questioning would not be fruitful. In fact, it would probably end with these two women walking out of the ER.

Standing up, I said, "Well, let's just check your tummy and see where your pain is located."

I walked over to the side of the table.

"Samantha, could you just lie back on the bed for me? Just get comfortable."

As I said this, her mother stood up from her stool and walked over behind me. She stood at my shoulder, watching.

Samantha dutifully followed my instructions and lay down on her back. Her hands were folded behind her head and she gazed at the ceiling, seeming quite relaxed.

"Okay," I said, lowering the sheet just enough to expose her abdomen. "Can you point to where it hurts the most?"

She was a slender girl and I immediately noticed a rounded protuberance just below her belly button. I glanced over my shoulder at Mrs. Stroud. If she had noticed anything her expression certainly didn't betray it.

Looking back at Sam I said, "Just show me where it hurts."

She used the index finger of her right hand to make large, circular motions over her entire lower abdomen. Not very helpful.

"Alright," I said, placing my left hand on her mid-abdomen with my right hand on top of it. "Tell me if this hurts."

Her abdominal exam did not reveal any significant tenderness, and she was unable to localize any point of maximum discomfort. I had been studying her face throughout, and she had remained passive and seemingly quite comfortable.

What I *had* found was a firm, nontender mass located just below her umbilicus and extending down into her pelvis. About twenty weeks along, I guessed.

After listening to her heart and lungs and completing my exam, I pulled the sheet back up, covering her. She grabbed the edge and again pulled it up to her chin.

"Well, Sam, I need to ask you one more time. Are you sure your periods have been regular and you've never been sexually active?"

"I thought we covered this, Doctor," her mother answered, obviously agitated. "If you're going to keep badgering her about this, we will leave right this minute. You heard what she said. She's never had sex with a man."

Sam continued to stare at the ceiling.

"Alright." I backed off. "Let's, uh, let's just check a few things. We'll get a CBC and a urine specimen. Then I'll be back with you."

Mrs. Stroud had stepped over to the side of the table and was patting her daughter's arm.

"And how long will all that take?" she asked impatiently.

"Not long," I answered. "Twenty, thirty minutes. And then we'll talk."

I walked up the hallway, considering my options here. We would get a pregnancy test, and I knew it would be positive. But how was I going to break that news to Samantha and her mother? They seemed convinced she was a virgin.

Stopping at the nurses' station, I put the chart on the counter and began writing. After jotting down a few notes, I looked over at our secretary.

"Marcella, could you get a CBC and a urinalysis in Gyn?" I asked her. "And a pregnancy test too."

"Sure, Doctor." She immediately reached out for the appropriate lab slips.

Jeff had been standing nearby and he walked over.

"What's goin' on? You seem a little bothered," he observed.

I told him Sam's story, and my dilemma.

"Well, you never know. Maybe they're telling the truth. Maybe she *is* a virgin, and maybe she's pregnant," he said, smiling. "Happened once before."

I looked at him over the top of my glasses. "Now wouldn't that be something?" I remarked, not amused.

It took forty minutes, but we had our answer. Samantha's CBC was completely normal, as was her urinalysis. And her pregnancy test *was* positive. The lab tech had walked the results around to the ER and as she handed them to me she said, "Turned positive almost before the drop of urine hit the card."

"Hmm," I muttered. "Thanks."

I picked up her chart, attached the lab results, and headed down the hall to the Gyn room. This was going to be interesting.

Jeff was pushing a wheelchair up the hall. The eighteen-year-old patient in it had sprained his ankle playing basketball and was on his way back from X-ray. As our paths crossed, Jeff asked, "Got your miracle?"

I returned his Cheshire-cat smile with a disapproving frown.

Mrs. Stroud didn't move from Samantha's side as I closed the door of the exam room behind me. She looked at me questioningly, while Sam just stared up at the ceiling.

"Sam, Mrs. Stroud," I began. "I think we have our answer." I held her chart in my left hand. Then I placed my right palm on top of it, staking my claim to the forthcoming diagnosis.

"And what is that, Doctor?" Mrs. Stroud asked.

"We've got our lab results back and they…" I started but then stopped, deciding on a different approach. "Sam, are you sure your periods have been—"

"Dr. Lesslie, that is just about enough!" Mrs. Stroud interrupted, with a subtle but unmistakable arching back of her shoulders.

I gave up. "Okay, okay. Let's just go over her lab studies."

Edging closer to Mrs. Stroud and the exam table, I opened the chart and began to review the lab-report slips attached to the top sheet of paper.

"Alright, this is her CBC, and it checks for any evidence of infection or anemia. And it's fine. And this," pointing to another slip, "is her urinalysis. No problem here—no blood, no infection. All that is good."

I took a deep breath before pointing to the next lab slip. "And this one, this is a pregnancy test. We checked, just to be sure. And as you can see, it is positive."

There, I had said it.

"What?" the mother exclaimed, grabbing the chart from my hands. "That's impossible!"

"Well, you can see for yourself," I explained, pointing to the appropriate box on the slip and the large "+" sign. "The lab doesn't make mistakes about this kind of thing."

"I don't care about the lab!" she shouted. "This has to be wrong. It must be someone else's report." She said this while looking down at her daughter. Sam continued to stare at the ceiling. It might just have been the exam room lighting, but she seemed a little pale now.

I stepped between Mrs. Stroud and Samantha and I patted the young girl on her belly and said, "Mrs. Stroud, I want you to feel something."

Slipping the sheet down far enough to expose Samantha's lower abdomen, I guided Mrs. Stroud's reluctant hand to the now-diagnosed gravid uterus.

"Can you feel this?" I asked, helping her fingers outline the grapefruit-sized growth. "This is her uterus, her womb. I would guess she is about twenty weeks pregnant."

Mrs. Stroud felt the firm, curved mass, and then pulled her hand away.

"Must be a mistake," she stated, shaking her head resolutely. "Sam is a virgin, and there must be a mistake somewhere."

Samantha continued to stare at the ceiling, and she again pulled the hospital sheet up to her chin.

"Doctor, this is impossible, and I, we—" Mrs. Stroud stammered.

She was struggling, and I interrupted, trying to help her. "Tell you what. Why don't the two of you talk for a few minutes. I've got a couple of things to do and then I'll be back. Okay?"

There was no immediate response, and I exited the room in silence.

At the nurses' station, Jeff stood waiting.

"What's the verdict?" he asked, with a smile.

"Well, Jeff," I answered. "I'd say the odds are getting slimmer. But there's still an outside chance we could have our Christmas miracle."

"Yeah, sure. I'd say those odds are between slim and none," he teased.

Twenty minutes later I handed the chart of an elderly gentleman in room 3 to our secretary. "We need some blood work and a chest X-ray," I told her. Fever, cough, shortness of breath—it would probably be pneumonia.

Just then, the triage nurse put another chart on the countertop, making a total now of at least eight new patients who needed to be seen.

That was enough. It was time to go and talk with Mrs. Stroud and her daughter. Doggone it, I needed to find out if I had my miracle or not.

As I closed the Gyn room door behind me, it was as if I had stepped into another universe. The atmosphere had radically changed, and instead of being met by a belligerent mother and an indifferent daughter, I saw the two standing before me side-by-side. They were smiling and had their arms around each other. Samantha was now dressed, and Mrs. Stroud had her pocketbook slung over her shoulder.

The door latch clicked behind me, and I waited for one of them to speak. It was Mrs. Stroud.

"Dr. Lesslie, I think we know what's going on now. And we think you are right. Sam *is* pregnant," she told me, smiling. I stood before them, tense, my head tilted to one side, waiting. "And," she continued, almost triumphantly, "she's not a virgin."

I slumped a little in my disappointment, but was careful not to lose my balance and fall over.

"So she's not?" I repeated, placing her chart on the exam table and thrusting my hands deep into my lab-coat pockets. I was struggling to find my comfort zone.

"No, and we figured out what happened," she went on. For the first time Sam was looking at me, as she listened to what her mother was saying. And there was the hint of a smile on her face.

"Yes," Mrs. Stroud went on matter-of-factly. "Back in the fall, maybe even late August, we had a family reunion out on our family homestead. About an hour or so from here, I'd guess, out in the middle of nowhere. Well, there were eighty, maybe ninety of us, with a whole bunch of youngsters. Teenagers too. Mainly we sat around talking and eating and the kids were swimming and fishing in the old pond."

She paused here and looked down at Sam. "It seems that Sam here and a bunch of her cousins went down behind the pond dam with some wine one of them had sneaked along with him. Before long, they were pretty soused. Right, Sam?"

Samantha only nodded and continued to look at me.

"Well, Sam says that was when Uncle Freddy came down and…well, he got her all alone and he had his way with her."

I was stunned. Not so much by what she was saying…I had heard much worse. But I was astonished by the manner in which she was saying it. Here was a woman who only a short time ago had been angrily confronting me for asking about the chastity of her daughter, and who now was calmly and coolly relating a tale of incest.

"That Freddy," she continued, "he's no good. He's part of that Tennessee side of the family. But not my family! He's on my husband's side. Or ex-husband, I should say. Anyway, he's no good, and it doesn't surprise me, not one bit. I'll have a word with him, you can be sure of that." She said these last words while patting Samantha on the shoulder.

I picked up the clipboard for the sole purpose of just doing something, anything. I didn't know what to say.

Mrs. Stroud came to my rescue. She took her arm from around her daughter, stood up straight, and asked, "So, Doctor, what do we do now? You think Sam's four to five months pregnant?"

We talked for a few minutes and I told them they would be given the name and phone number of an obstetrician in town. "You can follow up with him next week."

They both thanked me and walked out of the ER. I stood in the hallway for a moment, watching them leave. Poor Sam, and poor Uncle Freddy.

And what about my miracle? I guess I would have to wait.

As it turned out, that wait would be short-lived—only about six months.

"Dr. Lesslie, we need you in here *stat*." Jeff's voice was calm, but I recognized the tone. He meant business, and I immediately headed into the cardiac room. I had been walking up the hallway, talking with one of our surgeons about a young boy with appendicitis in room 5.

"What's the problem?" I asked, entering. My eyes were immediately drawn to the elderly man on the stretcher. I was not yet aware of the arrival of this patient and didn't know anything about him.

He was pale and obviously afraid. He looked from side to side, all the while tightly clasping the hand of a woman I assumed was his wife.

"Seventy-eight-year-old, history of heart disease," Jeff told me while starting an IV. "Came in from one of the doctors' offices in town. POV (privately owned vehicle). Blood pressure is 60 over zip."

Stepping closer to the stretcher, I reached out and put my hand on his uncovered shoulder. His skin was cool and damp to the touch. I glanced at the cardiac monitor and could see the telltale changes that suggested an acute heart attack. His rhythm was regular, about seventy a minute, and then...

"Jeff, get the defibrillator over here!" I turned to the woman standing at the side of the stretcher. "Ma'am, would you step back for a minute?"

She immediately released her husband's grasp and put her hand to her mouth, shrinking back against the equipment carts lining one of the walls.

Jeff was reacting quickly. He'd seen the same thing I had. The regular rhythm on the monitor had suddenly deteriorated into the spiked, choppy pattern of v-tach (ventricular tachycardia), an unstable and life-threatening electrical pattern. As confirmation of this change, our patient had turned dusky and was staring up at the ceiling, his facial muscles now lax. His low blood pressure must have dropped even lower. Then, just as quickly, we watched as the v-tach deteriorated even further. The tracing on the monitor screen told us he was now in ventricular fibrillation. His heart had lost all electrical organization and was simply quivering in his chest, a failing, purposeless "bag of worms." He was dying.

It was his good fortune this had happened in the ER, in front of us, and with the necessary equipment readily at hand to revive him. He would surely have been doomed had this happened at home or in his car.

I immediately applied the defibrillator paddles to his chest and shocked him once. Nothing. The monitor still revealed only the chaotic, undulating pattern of v-fib. I shocked him a second time, and then a third. Then...there was a faint *beep-beep-beep* coming from the monitor.

"Looks like he's back in a sinus rhythm," Jeff reported. And then pressing two fingers against the man's left carotid artery, he said, "And I can feel a faint pulse here. Sixty a minute, now seventy. Regular."

Our patient was responding. We watched as he took some deep breaths and began to look around the room, though still obviously confused. But his color was better and now he had a good, strong pulse.

One of our other nurses had come into the room and was now

leading the man's wife out into the hallway, where her daughter and son-in-law were waiting.

"I'll be out in just a minute," I said to his wife, "and we'll let you know what's going on. For right now, he looks okay." I looked up at the clock on the wall: 5:35 p.m. The next hour or so would be critical.

We quickly determined that our patient, Wylie Stanfield, was indeed having a heart attack, his third. While we were doing the necessary things to stabilize him, our unit secretary was making arrangements to have one of our cardiologists admit him to the CCU.

I learned that Wylie had started having chest pain sometime in the mid-morning. Prudently, his wife, Margaret, had become concerned. They drove to their family doctor's office and, after sitting for an hour and a half in the waiting area, were taken back to an exam room. Their physician was equally concerned and recommended they drive the fifteen minutes over to the ER for testing. Our triage nurse had observed the low blood pressure and his cool, clammy skin. Wylie was brought immediately back to the cardiac room, where Jeff had met him. And here we were.

"Jeff, you okay here?" I asked him. "I need to step out and speak with the family."

"Sure," he answered. "He looks pretty good now."

In the hallway, Margaret Stanfield anxiously waited with her daughter and son-in-law.

"Mrs. Stanfield, I'm Dr. Lesslie," I introduced myself, not having had the time to do this in the chaotic cardiac room. I then informed them of our diagnosis, our current plan, and the seriousness of his condition. The daughter, Theresa Streeter, and her husband, Mac, stood on either side of Margaret, their arms around her, holding her steady.

We talked for a few minutes until I was sure they knew what was going on.

"Can Mother and I go in there with him?" Theresa asked.

I thought Jeff had had enough time to get things straight, so I said, "Sure, but we need to keep him calm." I said this while looking at Mrs.

Stanfield. She seemed in control and nodded her understanding. The last thing we needed was for an emotional outburst to trigger another episode of v-tach, or worse.

The two women went into the room, and I was left standing in the hallway with Mac Streeter.

"What do you think, Doc?" he asked. "Do you think he can pull through this?"

"His chances are fair," I told him honestly. "After all, he is seventy-eight and he has a bad heart. We'll just have to see. Right now though, he's okay."

This seemed to satisfy him, and I turned, heading toward the nurses' station.

"Dr. Lesslie, do you have a minute?" he asked, tentatively. He was obviously concerned about something.

I stopped and said, "Sure. What's the problem?"

"Is there somewhere private we can talk?" He said this while glancing at the closed cardiac room door.

Curious, I looked down the hallway and thought a moment. Across the corridor, the ENT (ear, nose, and throat) room stood empty and dark.

"Let's go over here," I said, leading him away from the cardiac room.

I turned on the lights of the ENT room and closed the door behind us as we stepped inside.

I pointed to a stool in the corner of the room. "Have a seat, Mac. What do we need to talk about?"

Without any hesitation Mac Streeter began to tell me about the Stanfield family. "My first concern is for Wylie," he told me, "first and foremost," he stressed, looking squarely into my eyes. "And I don't want anything to happen here that might upset him and cause him trouble. I know he's not very stable."

And then he told me about the Stanfield's son, Phil. He was two years older than Theresa and lived with his wife and three children in a small town about an hour distant. Theresa had called Phil and told him of their father's condition. He was on his way, and his wife was staying at home with the kids. He would be arriving at the hospital shortly.

"The problem, Dr. Lesslie, is the relationship between Phil and his mother. They don't get along." I was soon to learn this was an understatement.

Mac explained that about five years earlier, something had happened at a family gathering. Words were said, misunderstood, and blown out of proportion. Phil and his mother were soon at odds and not speaking. It had been a trivial thing, but it soon became an open, festering wound. Attempts had been made to heal the break, but to no avail.

"You need to understand, Doctor, that while Margaret is a good woman, she is hardheaded. There's a side of her that's, well…She's just become bitter about this. She won't talk to Phil, won't answer his calls or return his letters. And she's put Wylie right in the middle of it."

"What do you mean, 'in the middle of it'?" I asked him.

"She won't let Phil talk to his father or see him. And if he does, she stops talking to Wylie and makes his life miserable. It's a real mess," he explained.

Mac and Theresa had tried to intervene, but unsuccessfully. Margaret was intransigent. The situation had worsened over the years and had taken its toll on all of them. Wylie had not been able to see his son or the three grandchildren, even though they lived only an hour away.

"I'm really afraid that when Phil gets here, we're going to have trouble," he continued. He shook his head. "Phil hasn't seen his father in five years. Or his mother. He's a good guy and I can't believe he would let anything blow up. But Margaret, on the other hand…I just don't know. We're going to have to keep them apart somehow."

What a mess. Wylie was barely clinging to his life, and this dysfunctional family dynamic was assuredly going to make things more difficult for everyone. Mac had been right to share the family skeletons with me. And we all had them. Some worse and some bigger than others, but they were there, usually hidden away. If a family thought itself immune to this, they weren't looking in the right closets.

We talked about the spiritual aspect of this situation. I opened that door with a simple question. "Have you and Theresa talked with a minister about this?"

Mac looked at me, seeming relieved I had been willing to ask this. He then told me he and his wife prayed about it every day. They prayed for reconciliation, and for Margaret's heart to be softened.

"We've talked with Margaret about this too, and she says she prays all the time about it and is just waiting for Phil to apologize. The frustrating part of this is that when Phil tries to apologize and make things right, she will have nothing to do with it. She says he's not sincere."

He paused and stared at the floor.

"You know, Dr. Lesslie, I believe in the power of prayer. I really do, and I've seen prayers answered. And I know the Lord can do anything. But when Theresa and I pray about this and put it in His hands, somehow…somehow…I know He can fix this, but I just can't see it happening. It's just so twisted and gnarly. We've tried everything, Theresa and I. And so has Phil. It's…just a real mess. And now this, with Wylie. I'm just afraid something bad is going to happen."

I assured him we would make every effort to keep Margaret and Phil apart, and to shield Wylie from any potential conflagration.

But it was not to be. As we stepped out into the hallway, I heard Mac moan behind me. "Oh, good Lord, we're too late!"

I glanced toward the door of the cardiac room and saw the back of a middle-aged man as he stepped into the room. Mac didn't have to tell me. I knew.

"It's Phil," he said. "Quick, I've got to get in there."

Phil was closing the door behind him, but I stopped it with the palm of a hand. Pushing it open, I stepped into the room behind him, along with Mac.

Phil never turned around. He stopped at the foot of the stretcher and looked down at his father. Wylie was lying there, quietly resting, eyes closed. Jeff was standing at the head of the bed, adjusting the rate of the IV fluids. Unsuspecting, he glanced over at the new visitor. Margaret and Theresa stood on each side of the bed, each gently stroking one of Wylie's forearms. They had looked up as Phil had entered the room. Theresa stood frozen, her eyes widening and her lips soundlessly parting.

Margaret stood completely still, staring at her estranged son. Then she patted Wylie's arm one more time and stepped toward the door. Mac and I were standing just behind Phil. I was blocking Margaret's exit, so I shifted toward Mac to get out of her way. She had reached the foot of the stretcher, when she stopped right in front of Phil. Their eyes met, and they both just stood there, staring at each other. Then she reached out and took her boy in her arms. And he wrapped his large arms around her, squeezing her tight.

"I'm so sorry," she sobbed.

His chest was heaving, and he struggled to whisper, "I'm sorry too."

And then there was silence, except for the *beep-beep-beep* of Wylie's heart monitor. And then the crying, from all of them. Mac and Theresa had watched in amazement, and now they huddled around Margaret and Phil, all of them hugging and sobbing.

Jeff looked at me, confused over what had just happened. He had no idea of the significance of this moment. Later, I would tell him.

There it was—my miracle. Wylie was lying quietly on the stretcher, not moving. But now his eyes were open and he was smiling.

I stepped out into the hall, wiping my own eyes and thinking of something that Mac had said earlier. He had put this whole thing in God's hands. But he had remained daunted by the enormity of the problem and its seemingly impossible resolution. *"The Lord can do all things, but…this one…I just don't know."*

Now he understood, as did I, that there is nothing beyond the power of God. There is no wall too high for Him to tear down, no situation too twisted for Him to straighten. He stands there ready and wanting to help, capable of softening the hardest of hearts, of resolving the thorniest of problems.

This, then, was my miracle. What greater wonder is there than the changing of a human heart?

Let the Little Children Come to Me

He took the children in his arms, put his
hands on them and blessed them.

—Mark 10:16, speaking of Jesus

I started medical school in the fall of 1972. In the last thirty-some years there have been a lot of changes in the field of medicine, both in the things we now know, and in the things we are able to do. For instance, some of the commonly used drugs then are no longer available, and some of the drugs we take for granted today were not even dreamed of then.

Back then as well, some things were only barely discussed in medical school, vaguely mentioned but not seriously considered. They were passed on as something to be aware of but not to spend too much time on. It wasn't that these weren't important topics, it was just that not much was known about them. One of these areas was abuse. First it was child abuse, later it was spousal abuse, and most recently, elder abuse.

In the mid-70s we were just getting a handle on child abuse. In fact, we didn't know how widespread the problem actually was, or the scope of things that were going on in our communities, both unseen and unheard. At first there was some confusion as to the nature of the problem, at least in the minds of some people. Was child abuse a disease, or was it a symptom of some larger disorder? Or was it a crime against a small, helpless human being? Those of us in the ER tended to see things as black-and-white. A six-month-old with two broken thigh bones from being thrown against the wall. A one-year-old with cigarette burns covering her buttocks because "she wouldn't use the potty." A three-year-old sexually abused by an uncle. These things were black-and-white.

As the magnitude of the problem became more apparent and the devastating consequences of child abuse became more evident, the thinking swung toward the ER view. There has been a much more organized and aggressive effort to detect abuse, protect the children involved, and prosecute those who are the abusers. Though human responses and actions are complex and multifactored, our primary responsibility is to protect our children. Those of us in the ER see ourselves as a line of defense, possibly the last and best hope for these young ones. Though it's true that the circumstances we encounter can sometimes be gray, they are too frequently black-and-white.

❦

It was 10:30 on a Friday evening. Summertime, and the day had been especially hot. During the past few hours we had seen our usual seasonal complaints: a few really bad sunburns, a four-wheeler accident with a broken ankle, and a few minor boating injuries. I had just finished suturing the fingers of a seventeen-year-old who had badly cut them while slicing onions at a cookout on the lake.

Standing at the nurses' station, I signed the teenager's chart and handed it to Jeff. He was the nurse on duty this evening and would be working with me until 7 a.m.

"Jeff, would you put a bandage on this girl's hand and remind her to come back in ten days for suture removal? I've talked to her about what to look for in case it gets infected, but you might want to go over that again. Thanks."

He took the chart and was about to speak, when suddenly the ambulance entrance doors burst open. Into the department ran a young woman, carrying in her arms a limp and pale baby. Probably six month old. The child's limbs flopped haphazardly as she ran.

"Help me, someone!" the young mother shrieked, stopping a few steps from where I stood. "Something's wrong with my baby! Please, do something!"

She couldn't have been more than sixteen years old. She stood in front of us barefooted and dressed in a dirty white halter top and red short-shorts. Jeff was the closest to her and she thrust her baby in his direction.

"Here—please do something!"

Jeff put down the chart he was holding, took the baby in his arms, and headed immediately to the major trauma room. I was right behind him.

He put the baby on the trauma bed and put his hand on the child's chest, checking for any cardiac activity. The baby was dusky and not breathing, and I immediately reached for our pediatric ambu bag. As I glanced in the direction of our crash cart, I noticed that the young mother had followed us. She was standing just inside the doorway, her arms folded tightly across her chest, biting her lip. Tears rolled down her cheeks. Behind her, not yet venturing into the room, stood a tall, slender young man, maybe in his early twenties but no older. He wore sandals, a pair of old blue jeans, and a T-shirt that read simply, "The Man." He was impassive, and leaned against one side of the door opening, chewing slowly on a drinking straw.

I turned to the task at hand, positioned the baby's head so we had better access to his airway, and began using the ambu bag to blow air into his lungs. I quickly checked to confirm his chest was moving up and down, indicating good air exchange.

When I touched the child's face and head, I immediately looked up at Jeff. His huge hand was encircling half of the baby's chest, and he was effortlessly compressing the heart between his fingers and thumb. Jeff's eyes met mine and his eyebrows rose slightly. I nodded. The small body was cold—the baby had been dead for a while. We were not going to save him.

One of our techs had come into the room, and I asked her to put leads on the baby for the cardiac monitor and to check a rectal temperature. This effort was futile, but I wanted the mother to know we were doing everything we could. And as cruel as it might seem, I wanted her to see the flat line of the heart monitor and understand her baby was gone.

The tech attached the leads and slipped the child's diaper off to check his temperature. There was a brief glimpse of his buttocks, and I noted several bruises on each one. The marks were of different sizes and different ages.

"94 degrees," the tech reported, placing the baby's legs back on the bed. As she turned the switch on the heart monitor, the screen flickered and then became clear. A horizontal green line appeared. Flat. No electrical activity. I made sure the leads were connected to the baby's chest and looked at the monitor again. Nothing.

"11:14," Jeff quietly noted.

I nodded, and put the ambu bag on the bed beside the baby. Jeff removed his hand from the child's chest and gently laid him back on the bed. I looked in the direction of the doorway.

"Ma'am," I addressed the young woman. I didn't even know her name. "I'm afraid your baby is dead. There is nothing we can do. I'm sorry."

She turned pale and sank to the floor. The young man remained standing in the doorway, now more aggressively chewing the straw in his mouth. It was at that moment his eyes betrayed him. It was only a brief flicker, but he had glanced down the hallway as if determining his best avenue of escape.

The mother began to sob now, covering her face. Our tech helped her to her feet. Looking at me, she said, "I'll take them to the family room, Dr. Lesslie. Is that okay?"

"Yes, please," I answered. "I'll be there in just a few minutes."

She led them into the hallway and as they turned to walk away, the mother covered her mouth with one hand. With the other she weakly reached out in the direction of the stretcher. She started to step back into the room, but the young man grabbed her arm and pulled her back into the hallway. And then they were gone.

I closed the door to the trauma room and walked back over to the bed. Jeff was cleaning and putting up the equipment we had used.

"Doesn't look like SIDS, does it?" he stated.

"No, it doesn't."

While Jeff worked, I began to examine the young child. I checked the long bones of the arms and legs for any obvious evidence of an old or new fracture. I didn't find any. We would have to get X-rays to be sure. And I examined the bruises on his buttocks we had noticed earlier. It was difficult to estimate their ages—probably any time over the past one to three weeks. But there was a relatively fresh one on his right buttock, and the outline of the fingers of an adult hand could still be discerned.

Jeff was standing behind me as I made this observation.

"That son of a b———," he muttered.

"Who?" I asked, turning and looking at him.

"That guy standing in the doorway. It must be the kid's father. And I'll bet he's been the one doing this. Did you watch him? He just stood there. Never so much as blinked the whole time."

I knew Jeff was probably right. But that would be for someone else to determine.

"Call the coroner and get him over here," I told him. "And call DSS. They need to get involved right away."

I turned to the lifeless body of the baby, and then thought of something. "And we need to find out if there are any other children in the house."

"I'll go tell Amy," he said.

While we had been talking, I had taken the ophthalmoscope from the wall and focused its beam of light through the pupil of the baby's right eye, adjusting the distance up and down until the retina came into clear view.

Jeff was halfway to the door.

"Come here a minute," I said to him. "Take a look at this."

He walked back to the bed and leaned down, peering into the scope as I held it.

"Do you see the retina there, the pearly white sort of background?" He adjusted his head until the retina came into view. "Yeah, I see it. And there's some blood vessels running across it."

"Right—those are supposed to be there, and they're normal. But take a look at about three o'clock," I told him. "Tell me what you see."

He continued to adjust his head, shifting a little to one side.

His head stopped moving. "Hmm. I'm not sure what I'm seeing, but off to the side the retina's all blotchy. It looks like clumps of blood or something."

"That's exactly what it is. That's blood on the retina. Retinal hemorrhages."

Jeff straightened up and looked at me.

"What does that mean?" he asked.

I examined the child's other eye, attempting to confirm that these findings were present on both sides. They were.

"It most likely means that someone has been shaking this baby. Shaking him hard enough to cause the vessels in the eyes to bleed. And when that happens, there is almost always associated brain damage. There is no way this child died from Sudden Infant Death Syndrome. It looks like he was murdered."

Amy had called the coroner and he was on his way, as was a representative from the Department of Social Services. She had also notified the police. I walked down the hall to the family room. I would need to try to help the mother, to answer any questions she might have, and to help her contact people if needed. And I wanted a few minutes to talk with the two of them.

I reached the closed door of the family room and stopped. Looking down at the child's chart in my hands, I scanned the record for the name of his mother. "Angel." And the baby's name was "Zack." I tapped lightly on the door, opened it, and stepped into the room. Angel was sitting on one end of the sofa, her elbows propped on her knees, her head in her hands. Her hair cascaded wildly about her face, hiding it, and her shoulders heaved with her sobbing. The young man sat on the other end of the sofa with his legs crossed at the ankles. His knees were nervously moving up and down. He slouched into the cushions, one arm resting on the back of the sofa. With his other hand, he twisted the straw that still hung out of his mouth. He looked up, and his eyes met mine as I entered.

I closed the door behind me and sat down in the chair nearest it. I looked over at Angel.

"Angel," I began. "I'm Dr. Lesslie. I'm not sure I was able to tell you that earlier."

At this she sat up and brushed her hair out of her face. Her eyes were red, and her face was swollen. She didn't say anything.

I looked over at her partner. "And you are…?"

He continued to stare at me, and from around his chewed straw I was able to hear, "Timmy." His legs were moving a little faster now, and he chewed a little harder.

"Okay," I said, turning back to the mother. "Angel, can you tell me what happened to your baby this evening? Tell me about his general health, or about any problems he has been having. And when did you know something was wrong with him?"

Angel wiped her nose with the back of her hand and said, "He was fine most of the day. And he's been a good baby, really he has. Never caused any problems. Then this afternoon, he got a little fussy."

She stopped and looked at Timmy. He was no longer staring at me, but was absently gazing at the ceiling in the corner of the room. He was now sitting perfectly still.

"I think he was getting a virus or something," she continued. "He seemed to have a little fever, and then he had some diarrhea. I didn't have any Tylenol in the house, so when Timmy came over, I went to the store."

"Are the two of you married?" I asked.

"No. But we're gonna get married pretty soon. I live at home with my momma, and Timmy helps out with Zack whenever he can."

"Is Timmy Zack's father?" I asked, glancing at him.

"Yes," she stated simply. His legs were moving again.

"Was your mother at home this evening?" I asked Angel.

"No, she works third shift. I called her a few minutes ago, and she's on her way."

She began crying again, and I handed her the box of Kleenex that had been sitting on the small table.

Timmy stood up, put his hands in his pockets, and in the small space available at his end of the room, he began to pace.

"And then what happened?" I asked her.

"Well, I was only gone a little while, maybe thirty minutes. The store is just down the street. Zack was crying when I left, but he seemed okay. And then when I got home…he…he…" She covered her face with her hands and began sobbing again.

"Is that when you noticed he wasn't acting right? That he didn't seem to be breathing properly?" I asked her.

She nodded her head, saying nothing.

I sat back and was silent for a moment. Timmy was standing still now, studying the fire evacuation plan that was hanging on the wall in front of him.

I understood what had happened to Zack. Timmy had been left with a fussy, crying baby, and he had snapped. It may not have been intentional, but the outcome was the same. He had picked the baby up and shaken him in order to stop the crying. It hadn't worked, and he just shook him some more. And he continued to shake him until finally he was quiet. And now it would be time for the police to take over.

But I wanted to ask them one more question. Some part of me wanted to see how they would respond.

"Angel." I addressed her, but I watched Timmy. "There are some bruises on Zack's bottom. It looks like he's been spanked, and pretty hard. And more than once. Have you noticed that?"

She sat up and stared at Timmy. "No. I, uh, I have seen…he does fall a lot, and, uh, I guess he, uh, he bruises, and…" Timmy stood absolutely still.

"Angel, he's six months old," I reminded her. "Are you telling me he's been walking?" I was becoming upset, and I knew it was time for me to leave. Her head hung down now, and she was silent. I didn't need to hear any more.

I stood and opened the door. Turning back to them, I said, "Just stay here. Someone will be with you in a few minutes."

I closed the door behind me and stood in the hallway for a moment. I was angry, and I wanted to go back into the room and grab Timmy by his throat and...But I knew I couldn't do that. It was my job to be an ER doctor. It would be someone else's to bring justice for this innocent, dead baby.

The sound of approaching footsteps drew my attention. I looked up and saw two police officers walking toward me.

෨෫෬

I will never forget the look in her eyes. It's been a little over twenty-five years, but I will never forget that look.

It was mid-December and a Thursday. Outside it was cold, and at six p.m., already dark. My shift would be over in another hour and I was trying to get the department in order for my replacement. So far, I was succeeding.

"Any big plans for Christmas?" Virginia Granger asked me. We were standing at the island of the nurses' station, just outside her office. She had been working on the nurses' schedule for the holiday, and I was writing up the chart of a guest in the observation unit. He had been practicing his seasonal celebratory imbibing.

"No," I answered. "Just plan to be at home with the family. It looks like you're having better luck with your schedule than I am with the docs'," I said, nodding at the clipboard in her hands. Her schedule was filled except for two openings. "It looks like I might be spending some of the holiday here," I added.

"Well, I hope not. Didn't you work last Christmas?" she asked.

I thought for a moment but couldn't remember. Holidays for an

ER doc seem to all run together. I was about to respond when movement in the triage doorway drew my attention. Seeing me look in that direction, Virginia turned her head as well.

Lori was walking into the department, leading a young woman who was carrying a large picnic basket in front of her. She held the basket with both hands, leaning over slightly and straining with the burden. Lori turned around and held out a hand to help, but the woman shook her head, refusing the offer. Lori caught my eye and with a slight nod, signaled she needed me. I watched as she led her patient around the other side of the nurses' station and into room 3, closing the door behind them.

Virginia had watched all of this transpire, and she said, "Dr. Lesslie, you'd better go see what Lori needs. We'll talk some more later." She turned and walked into her office.

I left the patient's chart on the counter and headed toward room 3. Something was amiss here, but if it was a significant emergency, Lori would have been more insistent in her request for assistance. And yet, my curiosity was piqued about the contents of that picnic basket.

Pushing the door of room 3 open, I found Lori standing in the far corner beside bed B. The basket had been placed on the stretcher and she was leaning over it, carefully removing a small baby wrapped in a dirty piece of army blanket.

"And when was the last time you said you fed them, Hope?" Lori asked the mother as I closed the door behind me.

Them? I stepped over to the stretcher and looked down. In the bottom of the basket was another bundle of what appeared to be a piece of the same dirty blanket.

"An hour ago, maybe two, I guess..." Hope answered, her voice faint and her tone almost apologetic.

I took my first real look at this young mother. She was tall, maybe five-eight, and slender. No—she was skinny. Her long brown hair was matted and dirty, and it hung unchallenged into her face. She stood hunched over, staring down at her babies. Her arms were crossed over her chest and each hand grasped the opposite shoulder. She was rocking from side to side. Her blue jeans were worn, and torn at the knees. The stained sweatshirt she wore couldn't provide much protection from the frigid December air. She had no coat.

I glanced down and noticed she had on sandals but no socks, and her toes were blanched and colorless from the cold. Lori interrupted my observations. "Dr. Lesslie." With her head she motioned toward the doorway. She was holding the blanketed infant in her arms.

"Hope, stand here next to your baby for a minute, okay?" she instructed the mother, nodding at the basket.

"Okay," was the faint response. Hope edged closer to the stretcher, her arms still crossed on her chest.

Lori and I stepped toward the door and then turned back toward the bed.

She leaned close and whispered, "When I called Hope into the triage area from the waiting room, another patient stood up and walked over. She pulled me aside and asked me if I knew anything about Hope. I told her no, and she proceeded to fill me in. She seems to know her, or at least to know *of* her. Hope has been on the street for a while, it seems. She was a straight-A student in high school. Then she met some guy, got pregnant, and her parents kicked her out of the house. They won't have anything to do with her. She's lived with some friends, but that hasn't worked out. And she's been in and out of the shelters, but she usually just wanders off. It's strange, but I don't think we've ever seen her here before."

"What's the problem today?" I asked Lori.

"It's hard to say," she answered, looking down at the bundle in her arms. "She doesn't make a lot of sense. I think her main concern is that the babies aren't eating. I just brought them straight back, so I really don't know yet. I haven't even taken a look at them."

"Alright, let's see what's going on," I said to her, stepping back toward the stretcher. "How old did she say the twins were? They are twins, aren't they?"

"Yes, twins. Girls. And she said they were eight months old," Lori answered.

Eight months? That couldn't be right. The baby Lori was carrying was tiny.

She placed the first baby on the stretcher and began carefully lifting the other one from the basket. I unwrapped the child that lay on the stretcher and was stunned. The girl was the appropriate length for an eight-month-old, but she couldn't weigh more than ten pounds. Later, after we weighed the two of them, we would learn that this baby weighed eight pounds two ounces, a full five pounds less than her twin. She was emaciated, and listlessly rolled her eyes in my direction. She was diapered in a dirty piece of old sheet, the corners held in place with duct tape.

Lori looked over my shoulder and gasped. Then she placed her bundle on the stretcher and quickly unwrapped the second tiny girl. She was naked, dirty, and barely breathing. Lori immediately reached over to the emergency button on the wall and called for help, her voice shaking.

We shifted into a different mode. The second baby was clinging to life, but just barely. Two other nurses came into the room and we rapidly proceeded to resuscitate her. In short order we had secured her airway and had an IV going, and she was under a warming blanket. She was stable, at least for the moment.

One of the pediatricians on staff happened to be in the hospital and had come to the ER to help with this emergency. He was going to admit the child to the Pediatric ICU and had called in one of his partners to help with the first baby. Though her condition was not immediately life-threatening, she was still in a lot of trouble. With things under control, I was able to step out of room 3 and back to the nurses' station.

Lori was standing at the counter, writing on the chart of the first twin. She looked up as I walked over, obviously shaken and upset.

"What do you think?" she asked me. "Is she going to make it? The second one? I've never seen a baby so skinny, so wasted. It's terrible."

Lori had three children of her own, a boy and two girls. A moment ago she'd been focused on the task at hand, an experienced and effective ER nurse. Now she was a mother.

"So tiny," she whispered to herself.

I sat down, exhausted. An hour of an adrenaline rush will wear you out.

"I'm not sure," I answered. "She has no reserve, no body fat at all. And what was her temp—96? I thought that's what you said."

"Yes," she replied. "It was 96.2. She was cold."

"Yeah, she was cold. That either means exposure or an infection somewhere. Neither of which are going to be good. Where is the mother? And what about the other baby?" I asked.

"Hope is in the family room with the police, and the other child has been taken to the Pediatric ICU. She was starting to perk up a little after she got warm and we gave her a little bit of a bottle." She paused, and then, "And I think someone from DSS is on the way to talk with Hope after the police are finished with her."

"Hmm. I doubt she will ever see those children again, assuming they live," I observed.

"You're right," Lori agreed. "But you know, Hope is pitiful. I think she's devastated by this, but something just isn't registering with her. The look in her eyes is really spooky. She's just not there."

"I know what you mean. Is someone from Mental Health going to come down and talk to her?"

"Yes," she answered. "In the next hour or so."

We sat quietly for a moment, each of us reflecting on the events of the evening. Then Lori broke the silence. "You know, I had just a minute to talk to Hope when I took her back to the family room. Right before the police got there. I asked her how long her children had not been eating, and she just sort of stared at me. Then she told me her milk had dried up about two or three months ago, and she had started feeding them whole milk. She said they seemed to like it fine, but they weren't getting as big as she thought they should. And then she just looked at me and said, 'I didn't know what to do.'"

We fell silent again.

The first twin spent three months in the hospital and then was placed in a foster home. It remains to be seen if she will develop normally. The second twin died after two days in the ICU.

I don't know what's become of Hope.

He took a little child and had him stand among them. Taking him in his arms, he said to them, "Whoever welcomes one of these little children in my name welcomes me; and whoever welcomes me does not welcome me but the one who sent me."

—MARK 9:36-37

10

The **Still,** Small **Voice**

*After the earthquake came a fire, but the LORD was not
in the fire. And after the fire came a gentle whisper.*

—1 KINGS 19:12

S he began to pace. It was about nine in the morning, and up until
this point she had been lying quietly. Back and forth across the
room she walked, her bloated belly attesting to the fact that she was
full-term, maybe a few days late.

I watched her closely, keeping a reasonable, unintrusive distance.
From time to time she looked at me, her dark eyes at once fearful
and trusting.

But something was wrong. I was an ER doc and had delivered
dozens of babies. And though I wasn't an obstetrician, I knew something wasn't right.

She made another pass in front of me, and when she turned I could
see a small foot beginning to protrude. Then she walked over and lay
down on her side, panting now. Above and behind her, the faces of
my four young children were pressed against the panes of the French
doors that led onto the screened porch. It was here that Scooter, our
miniature dachshund, had chosen to give birth to her first litter.

The kids' faces were excited and they looked on with anticipation.
Barbara stood above them, bent over, hands on her knees. She was excited
also, but this was tempered with a measure of anxiety. She was concerned
about Scooter, but she needed to protect her own litter as well. This was
the toughest but most important audience I had ever had.

Earlier that morning I had called our vet, expressing my concern about Scooter's slow progress.

"Don't worry," she had tried to reassure me. "Dachshunds are notorious for having difficult deliveries. It's their long, low backs probably. And don't be surprised if you have a stillborn pup or two. In fact, maybe half won't make it."

"What?" I had asked, incredulous. "What am I supposed to do about that?"

"Nothing," she had answered. "Don't do anything. Just let nature take its course."

I was silent, considering what she had just told me. It was contrary to everything in me to just stand by and watch.

"Call me if there's a problem," she added. "But everything should be fine."

She had hung up, and I returned to the porch and Scooter's pacing, and the faces of my children.

Scooter lay with her back to the French doors, only inches away from the glass. We had tried to make her as comfortable as possible on a couple of folded towels. I stroked her head and neck and tried to encourage her, regretting that I didn't speak dachshund.

The tiny foot was now more visible, and then there were two. But something wasn't right. They weren't moving. Maybe that was normal, but...And then there was the pup. He was tiny, wet, and covered with a glistening membrane that Scooter immediately began to gnaw and bite. I watched with amazement as she nudged and cajoled her firstborn, stimulating the pup and trying to tear away this covering. How did she know to do this? I knew it was instinct, but still, it was amazing.

I glanced up at the kids, and their eyes were big as saucers. They were pointing and giggling and bouncing up and down.

Then I looked at Scooter. She had lain back down, seemingly exhausted, still panting. Another foot began to emerge from her birth canal.

And then I looked at the first pup. He was lying on the towel, completely still, not moving, not breathing. I rubbed him, trying to stimulate the little guy, trying to get him to breathe. But nothing happened. He was dead. Glancing up at Barbara, I saw the look of concern on her face. And then I looked at the children. They were just staring, no longer giggling and bouncing up and down. They knew something was wrong.

I picked up the pup and moved him out of their sight.

Meanwhile, Scooter had delivered her second puppy. She was again nipping at the amniotic membranes and trying to stimulate this little girl. Nothing. Same as before.

To heck with this.

"Okay, Scooter," I calmly spoke to her. "Let me see what I can do here."

I wasn't sure how she was going to respond, but she just looked up at me with those large, dark eyes and cocked her head. When I reached over and grabbed the pup, she didn't whimper or make any protective movement. She just lay there, watching me.

The puppy was a tiny, lifeless form in my hand, barely covering my palm. I briefly looked up at the faces pressed to the glass in front of me. Their expressions were wide-eyed and confused. As I watched, my older daughter's lips began to quiver. That was enough.

Using my thumbs, I peeled the slick and still-wet membrane away from the puppy's head. Then—and I still can't believe I did this—I put my mouth over the pup's nose and mouth and sucked whatever mucus I could get out of her airway. I rubbed her between my hands to try to get some response, but still nothing. Then I put my mouth over hers again and inflated her tiny lungs. Four, maybe five breaths. And then with my right thumb, I began doing chest compressions. I had no idea how fast they needed to be, I just did what felt right. After about thirty seconds I stopped and watched. Still nothing. And then…her tiny head moved, just a little. And her mouth opened, and she took a breath. I rubbed her a little more, and she rolled her head again. This time, after another breath, I heard a faint yip. Scooter heard it too and looked up at me and then at her puppy. Then she lay back down on the towel. There was more work to be done.

The puppy was now actively squirming in my hand. She was going to be fine. I laid her on the towel beside Scooter and watched as she gamely tried to stand.

The sound of clapping and cheering came from the other side of the porch doors and I looked up. The kids were jumping up and down and yelling. And then I saw that my wife was crying. Without words, she thanked me and told me she was proud of what I had just done.

Scooter would deliver five more puppies. Only two responded to her maternal ministrations. The other three required the same resuscitative efforts, and did fine. We lost just one puppy that morning, the first one. And the last little girl pup, Ivey, was the runt of the litter. She would be a member of our family for almost thirteen years.

That was a bright and shining moment for me, one I will never forget. But the experience would prove to be something else, something much more consequential.

2:00 a.m. Two weeks later.

Sheila Rice had just returned from Radiology. She had taken two auto accident patients around for some X-rays. Nothing serious, just a few bumps and bruises. At the moment they were our only patients.

She walked over to the nurses' station and sat down beside me. "Doc, I'm gonna need some coffee here in a minute. How about you?"

"No, I'm fine right now, Sheila," I answered, not looking up from the day-old newspaper I was paging through. "Maybe later."

Sheila was one of our regular night nurses. For some reason, working the graveyard shift suited her home life. But most important, she was able to sleep during the day. She had been doing this for a long time, ten or twelve years.

I was always glad to have her working with me. She had a lot of experience in the ER and was cool and calm in an emergency. Maybe most significant, she was a great Password partner. When we had some downtime, usually three or four in the morning, a couple of the lab techs would come over and challenge us to a game. The outcome was always the same, and they'd limp back to their department.

"Well, I'm going to the lounge, so should you change your—"

She wasn't able to finish her sentence. The door to triage had burst open and one of our business office secretaries came barreling towards us, pushing a young Asian woman in a wheelchair.

"You better come get this one!" she yelled in our direction. "I think she's havin' a baby!"

Sheila was instantly on her feet. "Madeline, take her over there to room 1," she directed, pointing in that direction.

Madeline put her back into it and gained even more speed with the wheelchair. She wanted no part of this and was determined to make her own delivery as quickly as possible.

It was then I noticed a young Asian man following them. He spoke quickly yet quietly to the young woman, in a language I couldn't understand. She didn't say anything, just nodded her head.

Madeline and Sheila transferred our patient from the wheelchair to the stretcher, and then Madeline escorted the man out of the department.

"Come on with me," she said to him. "We'll need to fill out some paperwork."

I had remained seated during all of this. Sheila would call me when I was needed. *If* I was needed. Usually when expectant women came to the ER like this, a quick assessment by the nurse would determine they either were not in labor, or were in its very early stages. In either circumstance, we would immediately send the patient to the OB floor to be evaluated. Only very rarely, maybe once or twice a year, would we deliver a baby in the ER or in the parking lot. And that was fine with me. It was fun to do this every once in a while, but we really weren't set up to handle deliveries, and it was always a stressful situation.

"Dr. Lesslie, get over here now!"

It was Sheila, and I was immediately on my feet.

I reached for the curtain but Sheila pulled it open for me, grabbing me by the arm and pulling me into the room.

"Here, do your thing," she said. "This baby's crowning. I'll go and get the delivery kit."

"Are you sure?" I asked her, still hoping we could just send this lady upstairs.

"Well, you tell me," she answered. She stepped to the side of the stretcher and gently spread the woman's knees. The top of the baby's head, covered with thick black hair, was just visible. What I could see was about the size of a 50-cent piece.

Whoa! Now it was more like a tennis ball!

"Get that kit, Sheila, and hurry up!"

I grabbed some gloves from a box on the countertop and snapped them on. Looking up at this patient, I suddenly realized she hadn't made a sound, not a moan or anything. And I realized I didn't know her name.

"Ma'am, everything's going to be fine here, okay?"

Ma'am? Where did that come from? She just looked at me, no evidence of pain in her face, no sound coming from her lips. She obviously didn't understand what I was saying, so I just looked at her and nodded. She smiled, and nodded back at me.

Sheila came up behind me, tearing the blue paper from the delivery kit. With one foot, she pulled an instrument stand from the corner of the room to the end of the stretcher. Then, throwing the paper on the floor, she opened the kit and dropped it on the stand.

The contents of the kit were limited and straightforward. There was an umbilical cord clamp, scissors, a pile of gauze, a couple of small blue towels, ring forceps, and a suction bulb for the baby's nose and mouth. If we needed anything else, we could quickly find it in the supply closet.

Then the young woman made the first noise we had heard from her. It was only a faint grunt, but Sheila and I both reacted to it. I stepped to the side of the stretcher and Sheila moved closer to the head. Then she once again gently spread the woman's knees, softly speaking words of encouragement.

"There, there, honey, it's going to be okay," she reassured her. "Now don't start pushing just yet."

Too late. I could see one ear now. It was time to deliver this baby.

I reached down, located one shoulder, and delivered it with ease. The second shoulder quickly followed. And then in one slithery, slippery instant, the baby, a little girl, was lying on the stretcher between her mother's legs.

I felt an enormous relief. While reaching for the suction bulb to clear the baby's airway, I quickly glanced at our new mother's face. Her forehead was glistening with sweat and a smile spread on her face. Her eyes met mine and she nodded, still silent, still calm.

"What in the world is that?"

Sheila's shocked concern immediately drew my attention back to the baby.

"What are you talk—" I stopped mid-sentence and stared at the newborn. In the midst of the precipitous delivery, I hadn't noticed.

"What is this thing?" Sheila asked again, now pointing at something that completely enveloped the baby.

My pulse quickened and my chest tightened. The relief I had experienced just seconds ago was now gone.

And then an image flashed before my eyes and I suddenly remembered. *Scooter.*

The newborn girl was covered with a transparent, glistening sac. It was still wet and slippery, and it would prevent her from breathing. "Intact membranes" is the medical term. I had read and heard about such a thing, but with our modern delivery techniques this was a rare occurrence. Rarer still for an ER doctor.

Dropping the green bulb on the stretcher, I told Sheila, "Get me a number 15 blade." The calmness in my voice surprised me. But I *was* calm. I knew what needed to be done, and I knew how to do it.

Almost without looking, Sheila reached behind her to a shelf on the wall and quickly located the needed scalpel. She peeled back the sterile wrapper and held out the exposed handle.

Taking the blade, I quickly made a careful incision through the membrane, and peeled the glistening capsule away from the little girl's head. Grabbing the bulb syringe, I then suctioned her nose and mouth. Then, thankfully, the three of us heard her first loud, strong cry. She was as tough and resilient as her mother.

Sheila picked up the baby and used one of the towels to remove the remainder of the membrane and dry her off. The cord was then clamped and cut, and Sheila placed the girl in her mother's arms.

I slumped onto the stool at the side of the stretcher, enjoying this moment as the remains of the adrenaline surge washed through my body.

"Have you ever seen anything like that?" Sheila asked me as she gazed down at our new mother and child.

"Nope, sure haven't," I answered. And then I thought about Scooter again and the back porch. "Well, as a—"

"But how did you know what to do?" she persisted. "I've never seen anything like it."

I was thinking of where to begin when the voice of the unit secretary interrupted us. "Sheila, we got one out here," she called from the nurses' station.

"Hmm," she sighed. "Well, let me go see what that is. I'll call OB and have them come down and take this lady upstairs. I guess we should call the pediatrician too."

She walked out of the room, pulling the curtain closed behind her.

Later, when it was again quiet, I would tell her. And Sheila would understand. This was not some fortuitous coincidence. I believe Einstein was wrong when he said that "coincidence is God's way of remaining anonymous." Our Creator doesn't choose to remain unknown or in the background of our lives. He wants us to know Him, and to walk with Him, and to talk with Him. And if we will listen, He wants to talk with us.

For that, this night, I was grateful.

❧

Willis Stephens's head was trembling. Not badly, but sitting where

I was in the pew behind him, it was noticeable. Subtle, but noticeable.

I had been studying the back of Willis's head for the past minute or so, and a strange thought crossed my mind. *What if Willis were to collapse? What if right at this moment, he slumped over in the pew?*

We were at a point in the worship service where such thoughts were not too intrusive, or at least not completely disturbing. The organist was playing some quiet music, and my ruminations were not distracting me from a prayer or the sermon.

I'm not sure why I was considering this possibility. When my wife and I had slid into this pew, Willis had turned around and offered me a solid, firm handshake. He was almost ninety and still going strong. For all of the years we had been members of this church, Willis Stephens had been a fixture, a bastion of the congregation. He was known for his humor and generosity, and for his love of young children.

Yet on this particular morning, something caused me to consider the back of his head, this mild tremor, and what I would do should he suddenly collapse in front of me.

What would I do?

I glanced beside me at my friend, Francis Wood. He was about my age and strong and agile enough. But how would we be able to help Willis?

The vestibule just in front of us, to the right of the choir loft, would be the logical place to take him. There was enough room there, there was a telephone for calling 9-1-1, and we could close the door behind us to shield the congregation. But how would we get him there? I had dealt with this before, the issue of "dead weight." If a person completely loses consciousness and muscle tone, he or she becomes extremely difficult to pick up and carry.

Once, before I had learned to call for a male nurse or any available EMT, I had run out into the parking lot of the ER to help get a patient out of a car. The person had apparently had a heart attack and collapsed on the way in. A young female nurse and I had reached the vehicle, followed by another nurse pushing a stretcher. What ensued was something I never want to repeat. We tried to get a middle-aged man, weighing maybe two hundred pounds, out of the car and onto the stretcher. Arms and legs were everywhere. I thought I was in pretty good shape, but it was extremely difficult to maneuver the man onto the gurney. Somehow we managed to get this accomplished and get him into the ER. We were all exhausted.

Now, here was Willis. He probably weighed more than two hundred and twenty-five pounds. What would Francis and I do?

Then, like a flash, there it was, right in front of me: the "fireman's carry." That would do it. Let's see if I could remember...I would grab one of my elbows with one hand, and one of Francis's elbows with the other. He would do the same thing, creating a sort of chair seat made with our forearms. We would do this under Willis's slumping body and then be able to lift him with relative ease. Standing, we could then take him to the vestibule and carefully place him on the floor.

Having solved this dilemma, I relaxed just as our minister was getting to his feet and approaching the pulpit. I no longer noticed the continual shaking of the head in front of me.

We were a few minutes into the sermon when it happened.

There was a rustle of movement behind me. Not a lot, but just enough to distract my attention. And then there was a tap on my shoulder.

Turning to my left, I saw one of the young men of the congregation leaning into the pew behind me. He whispered, "Robert, we need you in the back. Something has happened to John Stanford."

I immediately stood up, and I looked beyond him to the back of the sanctuary. A few rows from the back wall, several people were huddled around the slumped-over body of John Stanford. A murmur of hushed voices began to sweep through the sanctuary, and somewhere in my subconsciousness I realized the minister had ceased speaking.

Making my way across the pew, I turned to Francis and said, "Come on, I'll need some help." John Stanford was in his mid-seventies and, like Willis Stephens, he must have weighed in excess of two hundred pounds.

My mind was racing as we hurried down the aisle. What had happened to him? Was he breathing? Had someone called 9-1-1? As we neared the back of the sanctuary, I watched as three or four men fumbled trying to get him out of the pew. This was not going to be easy, and I wondered how we were going to get him to the back of the church. We needed some space, and first we would have to get him out of the narrow confines of the pew. Then it struck me again: the "fireman's carry."

We reached his pew and I pointed to Francis and said, "Here, go in this row and get beside him." I made my way down the row behind John, stepping on a few toes as I negotiated my way.

Though John seemed completely unconscious, I quickly determined he had a pulse and was breathing. I said to the men standing around him, "Give us just a little bit of room." I then proceeded to instruct Francis in the carry. We fumbled with each others' elbows for a moment and then it all came together. It wasn't easy, but we were able to lift John and make our way down the pew and out the back to the foyer.

Gently, we laid him on the carpet and I again checked his pulse. It was there, but weak. He was pale, and his skin was clammy. Undoing his tie and unbuttoning his shirt, I asked Francis to raise John's legs to get more blood to his central circulation.

"Has someone called 9-1-1?" I asked the group in the foyer.

"They're on the way," came the response. "Should be here in about five minutes."

John was beginning to stir. His eyes opened, and he looked around him and then up at me. He was confused and afraid.

"John, everything's going to be okay," I told him. "Just relax and take some slow, deep breaths."

His color improved, and his pulse was stronger now. By the time the paramedics came through the foyer doors, John was talking and asking, "What happened?"

The EMS team had him on a cardiac monitor, an IV started in his right arm, and oxygen prongs in his nose within minutes. He was stable and was soon on his way to the hospital. He later told me that when visitors came to his hospital room, he would tell them, "The worst part of the whole thing was waking up on the floor and finding Robert Lesslie taking my clothes off."

As the ambulance siren faded in the distance, I turned to Francis and put my hand on his shoulder. "Thanks for your help. That was something, wasn't it?"

He was sweating, and I noticed that my shirt was soaked.

"Man, Robert, I didn't know how we were going to get him out of that pew. I'm glad you thought of...whatever it was we just did."

I knew then that, while those thoughts about Willis had been mine, they had come from some other place. I had never done the fireman's carry. I had never needed to—and to this day, I have never again performed it. On this particular day, however, John Stanford had needed some help, and I had been made an instrument. That was a humbling thought.

❧

2:30 p.m. Wednesday.

The chart of my next patient read,

> Brad Jenkins
> 42 year-old-male
> sore throat, cough, and congestion

The triage nurse had placed him in our ENT (ear, nose, and throat) room.

This should be straightforward enough, I thought. No fever. Blood pressure was fine.

With the chart in hand, I turned to walk down the hallway.

"You might want these," Amy Conners suggested to me. She was shuffling and straightening some medical documents. They were recent ER records, copies of visits, which we kept in the department. The file drawer they were kept in had a folder for each of the previous

31 days, allowing us to quickly retrieve the records of each patient visit for the prior month. We had a few "frequent flyers," and this system allowed us to better track these patients and their multiple visits.

"Looks like he's been here a half-dozen times in the past two weeks," she added, sliding the stack of records across the counter.

That was a little unusual, and before I went to the ENT room I needed to take a look at these.

Multiple visits represented a potential red flag. One of the cardinal rules in the ER had to do with return visits. It also had a lot to do with attitudes and assumptions. A dangerous tendency among inexperienced ER staff members was to assume that an unscheduled return visit was a nuisance and probably bogus. This tendency would lead to a superficial examination and evaluation on the return visit, which in turn would sometimes result in disaster. The returning patient might in fact have something serious going on that had been missed on the first visit. It sometimes required discipline to remain objective and dispassionate, but these patients needed to be approached with a finer tuning of one's clinical radar.

Amy was right. Including today's, I counted six visits for Mr. Jenkins during the past two weeks.

Hmm. On the first visit, I had been the examining physician. He had complained of head congestion, drainage, and a mild cough. My diagnosis had been an "upper respiratory infection," and he had been treated with a decongestant and cough medicine. I looked carefully at this note, making sure his vital signs had been normal, and that I had not missed any subtle bit of information. Everything seemed routine.

On the next visit, two days later at midnight, he had been seen by one of my partners. His complaint then had been of persistent cough and difficulty sleeping. His vital signs again were completely normal, and nothing suspicious showed up in his health history. On this visit, he had received an extensive workup, including a chest X-ray and blood studies. Everything was normal. My partner had made a diagnosis of bronchitis and had given him an antibiotic, covering any potential underlying bacterial infection. Again, everything seemed appropriate. And he had again been instructed to follow up with his family doctor should he not improve.

Mr. Jenkins had come back to the ER three days after that visit, stating that he was no better. His complaint was "cough, congestion, fatigue." The next visit was for "nausea," and the ER sheet from yesterday simply read, "no better." Each time, his exam had been normal and he was told to follow up with his doctor.

Maybe he didn't have a doctor. Maybe he didn't have any insurance or the financial ability to afford follow-up elsewhere. I glanced at the demographic portion of today's record and noted that he was employed by one of the large companies in town. He had listed his job title as "regional manager."

This was unusual. "Thanks, Amy," I told her, attaching these records to his clipboard under today's encounter sheet.

I closed the door of the ENT room behind me and stood at the foot of the exam table. Brad Jenkins was sitting on the bed, leaning forward with his arms outstretched and his hands grasping the edge of the thin mattress that provided only a modicum of comfort. His legs swung in tandem beneath him and he looked up at me as I entered.

He seemed comfortable enough, and in no obvious distress. He wore khaki pants, a light-blue button-down collared shirt, and a red tie. Nothing struck me as being out of the ordinary.

"Mr. Jenkins, I'm Dr. Lesslie," I perfunctorily introduced myself. "What can we do for you today?"

He stopped swinging his legs but maintained his posture, leaning over and holding onto the bed.

"I'm sure you're aware I've been here a few times recently," he began, nodding at the clipboard in my hands. "I'm just not getting any better. Still feel lousy, with some congestion and occasionally a little cough." He cleared his throat after this last statement. "And I understand you're the medical director here, so I just want to say that each time I've been treated, the doctors and nurses have been very professional. I have nothing to complain about regarding my treatment, except that I'm just not getting better."

Six visits in two weeks—and he sat here in front of me completely calm, and actually complimenting us. I looked down at his chart again, making sure he didn't have a low-grade fever, or a slightly elevated heart rate—something, anything, that might tip me off to a significant underlying problem we were missing.

"Well, thanks," I responded. "But our goal here is to make sure you're okay, and to try to figure out what's causing your symptoms. Have you had any weight loss, or night sweats? Any unusual changes in your appetite or daily routine? Any bleeding?"

The answers to these questions were all in the negative. I continued to probe for any possible clue to his problem, any bit of information that would lead me to a correct diagnosis. I would be happy for something that just pointed me in *some* direction.

Nothing. Everything seemed completely normal, except for this slight cough and sore throat. And even these symptoms, when pursued, were vague and nonspecific.

His exam was completely normal as well. Ears, nose, throat, heart, chest—all normal. His muscle tone and neurological exam were also normal.

I rubbed my chin and looked at the previous visit's notation. He had had a CBC (complete blood count) done then and it was completely normal. No evidence of infection or anemia, or any problems with his platelets.

"Well, Mr. Jenkins," I began, having exhausted any thoughts and ideas, "I don't see anything bad going on today. And I'm sorry I can't give you a specific diagnosis as to what's causing your problems. Sometimes it just takes a little while to sort these things out. I think the most appropriate thing for us to do is have you seen by one of the ENT docs here in town. Maybe in the next week or two. We can help you set that up."

I paused, waiting for a response. He said nothing, just looked at me.

"Does that sound alright?" I asked him.

He lowered his head and stared at the floor, nodding.

"Hmm. I suppose," he said. There was resignation in his voice, but no frustration, and certainly no anger.

"Okay then," I responded. "Let me get some paperwork together and we'll be right back. We'll help you get lined up with one of our specialists."

There was no response, and I stepped out of the room.

As I walked up the hallway, I realized I had no sense of closure with Brad Jenkins. There was a small measure of release. I had taken a complete history and performed a thorough physical exam. I had done my job. Yet there was no closure. Sometimes that just doesn't happen in the ER and you have to move on to the next patient. But this was somehow different. There was something else going on here and I couldn't quite name it.

At the nurses' station, I stood at the counter writing on Brad Jenkins's record. Amy was reaching into the referral file to retrieve the slip of paper with the names, addresses, and phone numbers of our ENT doctors.

"What's going on with him?" she asked. "Seems like a straight-up guy, don't you think? But with all these visits…"

"Yeah, he seems straight-up," I agreed. "But I don't know exactly why he keeps coming back. Everything seems okay."

I put my pen down, struggling with what to write in the box entitled "Diagnosis." What *was* my diagnosis?

Something was bothering me, and I didn't like the feeling. Trying to shake off this unwanted emotion, I picked up the pen again. Its point hovered above Mr. Jenkins's chart, momentarily suspended while a thought formed in my mind. I don't know where it came from, but as it crystallized I knew what I needed to do.

Putting the pen in my lab-coat pocket, I returned to the ENT room. Brad Jenkins was still sitting on the exam table, but now he was leaning back against the wall, his hands folded in his lap. I closed the door and walked over to the stool in the corner of the room. Sitting down, I looked at him and our eyes met.

"Mr. Jenkins," I began, a little unsure of where this would lead, but determined to take this course. "I need to ask you a couple more questions."

"Sure, Doctor, what do you need to know?" he responded flatly.

"On one of your previous visits, you mentioned you were having trouble sleeping. You told me that it was due to some cough and congestion—but how long has that been going on?" I asked him.

"Oh, a couple of months, I suppose," he answered. "Why?"

"And tell me about your daily routine. What do you do for fun?" I pursued.

A puzzled look appeared on his face, and he was obviously struggling for a response. "I, uh, I…you know, I really don't know," he finally answered.

After asking a few more questions, I came directly to my point. "Brad, have you ever had any problems with depression? Ever felt really down and disconnected?"

He stared at me for a moment and then looked away, hanging his head.

When he didn't say anything, I asked, "Have you ever thought about hurting yourself?"

Upon hearing this question, his chest heaved and he whispered, "Yes."

This was painful for him, but I had to go on.

"Have you thought about how you might do that?" I asked him.

He took a deep breath and looked straight at me. "Yes, I have. There's a .38 in my car, and I was planning on leaving here and driving out to the lake. I can't go on like this anymore."

Brad Jenkins told me about his failing marriage, his estranged teenage son, and the ever-increasing stresses of his high-profile job. His life was coming unraveled, and he didn't know where to turn.

"We're going to get you some help, Brad."

He would be admitted to the hospital under the care of one of the staff psychiatrists. While Amy was making those arrangements, I took

Mr. Jenkins's car keys and, with a security guard, walked out to the parking lot. We identified his car and unlocked the driver's door. I reached under the seat and felt the cold metal of a handgun.

God does speak—now one way, now another—
though man may not perceive it.

—JOB 33:14

11

Possessed

In the synagogue there was a man pos-
sessed by a demon, an evil spirit.

—LUKE 4:33

It was two o'clock in the morning, the middle of April. Remarkably, the ER was completely empty of patients. We had just discharged our last visitor, an alcohol-infused college student who had met a sidewalk up close and personal. He had sustained a laceration of his eyebrow, a badly swollen lip, and three fractured teeth. The morrow would be a tough one for him.

I was sitting at the nurses' station with my feet on the desk when the phone rang.

"Dr. Lesslie, it's for you," said Lynne, the night-shift secretary, handing me the receiver. "One of the ER doctors in York."

York is a small town fifteen miles from us, and they have a small but moderately busy ER. A phone call from there, especially in the middle of the night, was never a good thing. This would be no exception.

"This is Dr. Lesslie," I spoke into the receiver.

"Dr. Lesslie, this is Dr. Frost in York. I've got the duty here tonight, and I need a little help." He sounded young and a little perplexed.

"Okay. What's going on?" I responded, putting my feet on the floor and sitting a little more upright.

"Well, I've got a lady here, thirty-five or thirty-six, I think, and, uh, she needs some attention, and it's...it's more than we can provide here," he explained.

"What kind of attention?" I asked him, becoming curious and not a little apprehensive. "What's her problem?"

There was momentary silence.

"For one thing, she's crazy. I'm sure of that. But that's not her main problem," he stated with a newfound assurance. Yet there remained an undercurrent of consternation in his voice. Now I had a sense he was holding something back. When he had said "crazy," my mind had immediately shifted to a process that concluded quickly, with an acceptable and familiar disposition. The mental-health system in his county was a good one, and they were able to get people the psychological help they needed when they needed it. But he should know that. The York ER had its share of psychiatric emergencies.

"She, uh, she also has a medical problem that needs attention," he continued.

He waited for my response.

"And what is that?" I asked, now growing a little impatient.

"She swallowed her tongue," he stated flatly. "No, wait. She pulled it out first, and then swallowed it."

I sat there expecting more, but it was not forthcoming.

"She what?" I asked, needing clarification. "Swallowing your tongue" conjures up images of someone having a seizure and losing control of their musculature, with the attendant risk of their tongue limply falling back into the airway and causing a real problem. But of course no one "swallows" their tongue. And no one "pulls out" their tongue. It would be too painful and too bloody. This Dr. Frost on the phone must be nuts too.

"Just how bad is this injury, and how about her airway?" I gave him the benefit of the doubt.

"Oh, her airway's fine," Dr. Frost told me, now seeming more comfortable in this clinical dialogue. "And her tongue is pretty messed up, what's left of it. But it's not bleeding too much. She, uh, she won't let me get a good look. But she's breathing just fine."

I thought for a moment. "Well, it sounds to me like she needs an ENT doc, or maybe an oral surgeon. Have you called anybody?"

The medical community in York was rather limited, with mainly family practice physicians on the staff. There were no specialists, and patients needing the services of one were usually sent to Rock Hill.

"I tried a couple up your way, Dr. Woods and Dr. Smith, but they weren't interested," he told me. "They won't accept her in transfer. No luck there. They both thought she should be seen by someone from mental health first, and then some kind of decision could be made."

He should be able to handle this, but I sensed he was trying to make his problem mine, and I was determined not to let that happen. This was my chance. I would advise him to pursue this last option, the psych referral, and let them resolve his dilemma.

Before I could speak, he continued. "And I called mental health, but they said her medical problem had to be stabilized before they would get involved. See the predicament I'm in?" He was trying to hand this off to me, but I would have none of it.

"Well, it does sound like a tough situation. Have you tried anyone in Columbia or Charlotte? Maybe someone there would be able to help out. And what about your medical doctor on call in there? Maybe the patient has a family physician you could call?"

"Nope, I've tried all of those," he said. And then here it came. "I was hoping that—"

I interrupted him. "My advice would be that you keep trying. Or maybe keep her stabilized until morning, and see how things shake out then. It's usually easier to make some of these tough dispositions in the light of day," I advised him. Anticipating a rebuttal, I continued, "But I don't think we can help you here. It sounds like you've done everything we would do. I'd just keep trying and, well…good luck."

I had no qualms about my response to his predicament. He was working as an ER doctor and should be able to take care of this situation. Besides, there was an unspoken law among the brotherhood of ER docs: "Thou shalt not dump on one another." And this would really be a dump.

There was silence on his end of the phone. And then a resigned, "Okay, I'll keep trying and see what I can come up with. Thanks." He was clearly disappointed as he hung up.

Lynne looked up at me. "What was that all about?" she asked.

"The poor guy in the York ER has a real mess on his hands. He's got a psych case, and he's not sure how to handle it. I guess he was looking for us to bail him out, but this is something he needs to handle on his own. Hopefully."

"Hmm," was Lynne's response as she resumed work on her crossword puzzle.

I went to our office for a cup of coffee and to continue work on next month's schedule. It had the promise of being a quiet night, one to be appreciated, and one that presented an opportunity to catch up on some paperwork.

Thirty minutes later I walked up the hall to check on things at the nurses' station. Kathy Neal, a recent graduate from nursing school, was restocking the minor trauma room as I walked by.

"Still quiet," she said, clearly relieved, and certainly hopeful. She had been in the department for only three weeks and was still green. She was maybe a little too sensitive, but the consensus was she would be a good ER nurse. She would need some experience, but the ER of Rock Hill General would provide that pretty quickly.

"Yeah," I responded. "It's been a good night." I looked at my watch. 2:40 a.m.

At the nurses' station, Lynne had set aside her puzzle and was organizing her work area, making sure the next shift would have plenty of the multiple forms and reports necessary to carry on the business of the unit secretary.

The ambulance doors suddenly opened, activated by weight on the outside floor mat. Reflexively, I glanced in that direction.

"Are we expecting something?" I asked Lynne.

"Not that I know of," she answered, looking up at the entrance. "Nobody's called me."

Through the doors came a stretcher guided by two EMTs, one

holding onto each end. I immediately recognized the two young men and their uniforms. They were with the York Rescue Squad.

On the stretcher, sitting up and straddling the gurney with one leg dangling over each side, was a young woman. She looked angry, and her lower lip was protruding as she stared straight ahead. She seemed completely oblivious to her new surroundings. Her hands were folded in her lap, and on the top of her head, falling almost into her eyes, was a tattered and soiled blue rag. It appeared to be some sort of a small towel.

"Whatcha got?" I asked Danny, one of the EMTs. I already knew the answer to this obligatory question. *Dr. Frost.*

Lori had heard the ambulance doors open and had come back into the department from triage. She was having the other EMT wheel the patient to room 5.

Danny stopped at the nurses' station, releasing the stretcher to his partner. He had a clipboard tucked under his arm, and he placed it on the countertop. He opened the metal flip-top and began making a few notes.

"Well, Doc," he began, "got a call from the York ER to bring this lady up this way. Dr. Frost said he had talked with you and you would be expecting her."

I felt my face flush, but didn't immediately say anything. *Don't shoot the messenger* and all that. Danny had nothing to do with this. He was just doing his job. My first instinct was to pick up the phone and blast this young Dr. Frost. But what good would that do? Nothing, at least not at this point. I couldn't turn the stretcher around and send this woman back to York. She was mine now. But I would be having a chat with Dr. Frost in the not-too-distant future.

Danny told me the story, repeating most of the information I had been given earlier. But then he added some information he had gathered from the sheriff's deputies who had been in the York ER with this woman.

"It seems, Doc, this woman has a long mental history. She and her two sisters had been causin' some disturbances in town over the past couple of days. Approachin' people on the street and threatenin' them with voodoo stuff and whatnot. Went into one of the stores downtown and started singin' and chantin'. This patient here, Ethel, seemed to be the worst. Finally, the deputies locked 'em all up. Sometime yesterday, I think. And that's when it got weird."

He paused, glancing over to room 5. Lori and the other EMT had transferred Ethel from the rescue squad's stretcher to our bed. She seemed to be peaceful enough at this point, sitting calmly, her arms still folded, her blue towel securely in place. Kathy Neal had stepped into the room and was watching from a safe distance.

Before Danny started again, I spoke to Lynne. "Go ahead and call Security. We'll need someone to stay with her until we can figure out what to do."

I turned back to Danny, and he continued. "One of my friends at the jail told me he locked the three sisters in the same cell, and they just huddled up in a corner, and were just rockin' back and forth and mumblin' stuff. Then things got real quiet, and he went back to take a peek, to make sure everything was okay. Man, that must have been when it started. Ethel here, she had her fingers in her mouth, like she was trying to get somethin' out. And she was. She was pullin' out her tongue, piece by piece with her fingers. And she finally pulled it all out, every bit of it."

He stopped, shaking his head.

"She what?" I asked. Now this was a little far-fetched. I had seen a lot of tongue injuries in my years in the ER. Kids falling, landing on their chins, and splitting the tips or sides of their tongues. I had even had an eighteen-year-old who came in one night telling me his girlfriend had gotten mad at him, then professed forgiveness and kissed him. During this kiss she had bitten off and swallowed the tip of his tongue. But it had only been the tip, a dime-sized piece, and it had only required a couple of stitches to repair. But ripping out your own tongue with your fingers? Impossible.

"Yep," Danny went on. "Every bit of it. Gone. And the funny thing, Doc, is it didn't even bleed very much. I woulda thought she woulda bled like a stuck pig, but she didn't. I guess it clotted off or somethin'."

"Why in the world would she do something like that?" I asked him, studying Ethel from a distance. She had begun to slowly and rhythmically rock forward and then backward.

"Her sister told the deputy she was tired of evil spirits speakin' through her and was gonna put a stop to it. And that's why she's got that nasty towel on her head—to keep the spirits from getting in. Just try to take that thing off. She'll snatch your hand quick as a flash."

"Hmm," I mused. This was pretty interesting, even though I doubted the seriousness of her tongue injury. No one would be capable of pulling their own tongue out. But the fact remained that I would have to sort this thing out and find something to do with Ms. Ethel.

"Well, thanks, Danny. And if you find yourself in the York ER again tonight, thank Dr. Frost for me."

"Sure thing, Doc," he replied. His face showed puzzlement over this last remark.

A security guard was walking up the hall as I approached room 5. In this case, the term may have been a little self-contradictory. This seventy-plus-year-old gentleman might be a guard, but he didn't look too secure, nor did he inspire much of a sense of security. Our hospital was not unlike many others. In their attempt to hold down expenses, they hired the cheapest security group they could find, which meant we usually had retired individuals, unarmed and untrained. But they had spiffy uniforms. Ed was one of our regular night-time guards, and he was quiet and pleasant enough. But on the occasion of a real problem in the department he had the habit of disappearing. Hopefully, watching Ethel would not be too taxing a job for him.

"Ed, pull up a chair here and just keep an eye on her," I said, leading him into room 5 and pointing to a corner of the room.

Lori was taking Ethel's blood pressure as I walked over to the bed.

"Ms..." I paused, glancing at the clipboard lying by her side, "Jones.

I'm Dr. Lesslie. We're here to help you tonight, and to see what we can do for you."

She didn't respond. She just kept rocking and staring straight ahead. I glanced at Lori and she looked at me, shaking her head.

I needed to try. "So, Ethel, let me take a look at your mouth."

To my surprise, she stopped rocking, turned her head toward me, and opened her mouth. I mean *really* opened it. Not wanting to lose the opportunity, I grabbed the wall-mounted flashlight and took a look.

I was shocked! It takes a lot to surprise me, but I was truly taken aback.

"Holy—" I began, but stopped, catching myself. I was still the doctor here, and needed to at least appear calm and in control.

But, "Holy smoke," I muttered to myself. "It *was* gone!" Her tongue was completely ripped out. I leaned in and took a closer look. It had been torn out to its very root. There was nothing left, just a nub at the back of her mouth. To my amazement, there was no bleeding, just a few clots covering the stump.

Lori was peering over my shoulder and I heard a faint gasp. We looked at each other, but neither of us said a word.

I stood up and replaced the flashlight in its holder. Ethel closed her mouth and resumed her upright posture, staring straight ahead but rocking in a different direction now, from side to side.

I walked out of the room, Lori beside me. Ed was seated in the corner, his legs crossed and his arms tightly folded across his chest. He was a comical vision. His bright-red baseball cap was askew, its rolled bill pointing to his left shoulder. And his narrow navy-blue tie had flipped over and settled on the right side of his chest. Yet he was deadly serious about his assignment, not taking his eyes off his charge as he began his vigil.

"Wow," Lori said. "I've never seen anything like that."

"I don't think I have either," I agreed, stroking my beard and beginning to wonder just what I was going to do with this woman.

Over the next hour, the prospects of finding a reasonable solution to this dilemma became dimmer and dimmer.

I made a few phone calls to our local docs, to see if one of the ENT specialists would take a look at this woman. The doctor on call had already been contacted by Dr. Frost and told me the same thing he had told him. "Robert, it sounds like this lady needs to see a psychiatrist. That's probably where you should start."

And you can imagine what the psychiatrist offered. "Robert, this is a medical problem first. Get her squared away with that, and we can take a look at her later on. And good luck."

Yeah. Good luck.

I passed all this on to Lori and asked her to be considering what we might be able to do. For the moment I was stuck. But at least Ethel was calm, and she was stable. There was absolutely no bleeding from her mouth.

Ed had given Ethel a small pad of paper and a ballpoint pen. "Figger she can't talk to us, and if she needs somethin', she can just write it on that paper there." He pointed to the pad that lay at the foot of the stretcher, seemingly unnoticed by Ms. Jones.

It was then that Ethel started. I was standing at the nurses' station and absently looking in her direction. Slowly her right arm went into the air and her torso turned toward Ed. Her index finger was extended, curled, and began to slowly make circles in the air. Suddenly, she pointed directly at Ed, and her head began shaking violently. Her eyes were wide open, and she seemed to be mumbling something, though it was completely incoherent. I thought our security guard was going to fall on the floor. There was a look of complete and paralyzing fear on his face. He had pushed his chair back against the wall as far as it would go, but that wasn't far enough. He slowly stood and edged sideways out of the room, never taking his eyes off Ethel. And she never took her eyes off him. She tracked him out of the room with her finger, her head shaking, her silent lips working feverishly.

"She's puttin' some kinda voodoo thing on me, Doc. That ain't right. I don't got to put up with this. No, sir," Ed told me, stepping out into the hallway. He hitched up his pants and said, "I'll just stand right over here, if it's all right with you." He quickly walked around the corner, out of Ethel's gaze, and stood leaning against the wall.

Lori had stepped into room 5 and was trying to calm our patient. She patted her gently on her shoulder, and in a moment, all was again under control. Ed stayed in the hallway, out of Ethel's sight.

It wasn't long after that Ethel picked up the pad of paper and began writing. I was tempted to ask Ed to see what she had written, but thought better of it.

I walked over to her, and glanced down at the pad. "Bathroom."

"Lori," I called out. This was something I couldn't help her with.

A few moments later, Lori was leading Ethel down the hallway, and it was quite a sight. Lori held her by the elbow, or I guess it was her elbow. Ethel was a great moving mound of sheets which had been indecorously draped around her. She was barefooted, shuffling along and looking from side to side. On top of her head was the blue towel.

I watched as they approached Ed, who pressed himself into the wall as they passed, his chin tucked into his chest. I chuckled at this, and then was startled by a scream and the loud clamor of metal pans banging and clanging on the floor. I could see the shiny stainless steel basins and bowls as they cascaded out of the ENT room.

It seems that Kathy, our novice nurse, had been working in this room, restocking and straightening up. She'd been carrying an armful of pans when she stepped to the doorway, looked up, and saw Ethel standing in front of her. That was all it took. She had dropped everything she was carrying and run down the hall. Later, she would confess she had wet her pants.

At 5:45 a.m., Lori struck upon the idea that would save us. "Why don't you see who's on call for ENT at one of the hospitals in Columbia, and see if they will accept her? Maybe the doctor in York didn't really call anybody down there."

"Hmm, that's a good idea," I responded, glad for any help from any quarter. Dr. Frost had said he'd called some docs in Columbia, but given his irresponsible actions, there was a good chance he hadn't. Now I was *hoping* he hadn't.

"Lynne, why don't you call down to Columbia General, talk to the secretary in the ER, and see who's covering ENT for them tonight. See if you can get them on the phone."

Fifteen minutes later, the phone rang. Lynne answered. "Dr. Lesslie, it's for you. A Dr. Bissel in Columbia."

I had never heard of a Dr. Bissel, but it didn't matter.

I picked up the receiver. Dr. Bissel was on call for his ENT group, and I explained Ethel's circumstances to him. I told him she clearly had a psych problem, but the overriding concern now was the injury to her tongue. I'm not sure he was completely awake, because he agreed to accept her. He instructed me to have her sent to the ER at Columbia General and he would take care of things from there.

"Thanks a lot, Dr. Bissel," I told him. "We'll get her on the road."

I hung up the receiver and looked at Lynne and Lori. "Whatever happens, *do not* answer that phone. If Dr. Bissel wakes up and changes his mind, I don't want to know about it. Let's get her on the interstate as fast as we can."

"I've already called EMS," Lori told me.

Twenty minutes later, one of our paramedic teams had transferred Ethel to their stretcher and was wheeling her out of the department. They came by the nurses' station, where I stood with Lori, and paused while she finished completing the required transfer papers.

I looked down at the sad figure on the stretcher. What circumstances had brought Ethel to this point? Was it no more than faulty neural connections in her brain? Or were she and her sisters right about the demonic spirits? Whatever the cause, the effect was a destroyed life. There was a darkness here, and I sensed it was more powerful than any medication we could offer her.

Lori folded the completed documents. She put them in a large envelope and handed this to the paramedic standing at the head of the stretcher. Then she said, "Good night, Ms. Jones. I hope that everything goes well for you."

Ethel didn't respond. She just stared straight ahead, wrapped in a hospital sheet, the blue towel still on her head. Then she looked at me and held out her hand. She opened her fingers to reveal a crumpled, sweat-soaked piece of paper. I stared at it. At first I didn't move. She nodded, and thrust her hand closer to me. There was nothing to do. I took the piece of paper.

The stretcher was moving toward the ambulance entrance. Ethel twisted her torso and stared at me, her eyes large and unblinking.

Unfolding the piece of paper, I read, "It will turn green and fall off."

Somehow I knew she wasn't talking about my nose.

Looking up, I saw the doors closing behind Ethel and her entourage, and then they were gone.

Everyone in the department was going about their normal duties. I didn't say anything to anyone, just dropped the scrap of paper into a nearby trash can.

Voodoo? Black magic? Demon possession? Mental illness? Nonsense?

You'll have to decide for yourself from what I've told you.

But I know what I think.

12

If **Tomorrow** Never **Comes**

*You do not even know what will happen tomorrow. What is your
life? You are a mist that appears for a little while and then vanishes.*

—James 4:13-14

In his song "If Tomorrow Never Comes," Garth Brooks follows
that phrase with "would you know how much I love you?" That's a
very pointed question. If there were no tomorrow, would we have said
everything we need to say and done everything we need to do?

Probably not. Most of us stay focused on tomorrow and not enough
on today, and things go unsaid and undone. That reality comes crash-
ing home almost every day in the ER.

The light turned green and Jill Evans pulled out into the intersection,
turning left. She was driving safely but was a little distracted, still upset
about the argument she had had with her husband last night. She was
trying to remember how it started. Dan came home late from work
and was going through the mail. There was the phone bill, the electric
bill, and then the credit-card statement. That's what had done it. He
had exploded when he opened the envelope.

She didn't see the pickup truck as it ran the red light, its driver
looking down to locate a dropped cigarette. He never applied his
brakes and the truck T-boned Jill's small sedan at full speed, caving
in the driver's side and flipping the car over. When the police got to
the scene, the pickup driver was standing by the crushed hood of his

truck, rubbing his bruised and scratched left shoulder. Jill was on her way to the ER.

Jeff was waiting for the EMS team as they came through the ambulance doors.

"Bring her in here," he told them, standing in the doorway of major trauma. We had activated our trauma response team and they were on their way in. I followed Jill's stretcher into the room.

There was a flurry of activity as we moved her to the bed. She had one IV in place and another was being started. Blood was being drawn, and two X-ray techs were shooting films of her neck and chest.

Denton Roberts and his EMT partner had told us of the scene and of Jill's initial condition. She was unresponsive and had an obvious head wound and a crushed left chest wall. They had managed to secure her airway with an endotracheal tube and maintained her blood pressure with rapidly administered IV fluids. Her condition had worsened when she got to the ER. Her blood pressure was falling, and she was exhibiting signs of a devastating brain injury.

"Does she have any family?" I asked. I glanced down and saw that the fingers of her left hand were mangled and obviously broken. And I saw her wedding band.

"Her husband's on the way," Denton answered. "He was at work and should be here any minute."

We continued to work with Jill, inserting a chest tube to re-inflate her left lung and stabilize her chest. And we called Radiology to arrange for an urgent CT scan of her head. The on-call neurosurgeon and general surgeon were on their way down.

Virginia Granger pushed the trauma room door open and walked over to the stretcher.

"Her husband is here," she told me. "He's in the family room and only knows his wife was in an accident. He doesn't know how bad she is."

Sam Wright, our general surgeon, had followed Virginia into the room. As he began his examination of Jill, I filled him in on what had happened thus far.

Then I turned to Virginia. "Okay, I'll go talk with her husband. Do we know his name?" I asked her.

"Dan Evans," she answered. "And he's by himself."

It was another lonely walk down the hall to the family room. Jill wasn't dead, but her prognosis was very grave. Sam Wright had agreed with my assessment. "I don't believe she's going to wake up, is she?" he had observed. Her head injury was extensive, and I had to agree.

Dan Evans was on the sofa in the family room. He sat there with his head hanging down and his hands clasped together. He looked up as I entered, an expectant expression on his face. He was in his late twenties and was dressed in a dark business suit and red tie.

"Are you here to tell me about Jill?" he asked me.

I walked over to the chair beside him and sat down. "Yes, I'm Dr. Lesslie. And you are Jill's husband?"

"Yes, yes. I'm Dan Evans," he answered. "How is she? When can I see her?"

I held her chart in my hands and was considering how to begin this when he said, "We, uh, we had a big fight last night. It was about something stupid. A credit-card bill, I think."

He put his hands on his knees and stared at the floor, shaking his head.

"It was really stupid, something so small. But I blew it out of proportion, and we started yelling at each other. We didn't even talk this morning. Hey, I didn't even see her before I went to work. And now this."

He paused and I said, "Mr. Evans—"

He interrupted again, as if I were not in the room.

"I didn't even say 'goodbye,' or 'I'm sorry,' or anything. I just got up and got dressed and got out of there." He looked up at me and stopped shaking his head. "You know, we have a rule, Jill and I. We made a promise when we first got married that we would never let the sun set on our anger. I think it comes from the Bible, or somewhere. And most times we're able to do that. One of us will remember our rule and remind the other, and we'll take a minute and figure things out. One time we…" He seemed to lose his focus for a moment, gazing at the chart in my hands.

Then he looked up again. "Don't you think that's a good rule?" he asked me. "Anyway, last night, I didn't think about it and neither did Jill. We just yelled at each other, and then I went in the bathroom to take a shower. When I got out, she had gone into the guest room and locked the door. I went to bed, and that was it."

When he paused this time, I knew he had finished. But I waited a moment, just to be sure. He sat before me, silent, his eyes searching my face.

"Dan, let me tell you about Jill…"

❧

Dr. Simmons was in the middle of his examination when he glanced over at his nurse. With a barely perceptible tilt of his head, he silently signaled for her to step over behind him. He shifted back and to his left so she could see through the pelvic speculum. Her eyes widened as she looked at the golf-ball-sized ulcerated mass that had engulfed this young woman's cervix. She looked at Dr. Simmons in disbelief and shock.

"Now tell me again, Christy," he said to the twenty-eight-year-old lying on her back on the exam table. "When did this problem start?"

Christy McKenna repeated her story. She had noticed some bleeding a few weeks ago, unrelated to her periods. At first it had not been very much, but over the past few days it seemed to be getting worse. She didn't have any pain and had no other symptoms.

"And when was your last Pap smear?" he asked.

She was silent, and Dr. Simmons's nurse looked up at her. Christy had flushed and avoided her eyes.

Christy had grown up in Rock Hill and had left town to attend college. She had been offered a job right out of school and stayed in that same community. She hadn't established a relationship with any physicians there. She had come home to spend a few days with her folks and to see Dr. Simmons. He had been her Ob-gyn doctor since she was seventeen.

"I've been real busy lately, Dr. Simmons," she told him. "You know I stayed in Columbia after college, and with my new job...I just haven't had the time. I know that's not a good excuse, but I've just been going in too many directions."

"Uh-huh," he murmured. "So, when do you think your last exam was?" he persisted.

"It would have been, uh, probably the summer after my sophomore year. I think that's when I was last here," she answered.

"Hmm, that would be six or seven years," he calculated.

"I didn't realize it had been that long, but I suppose you're right," she replied sheepishly.

"Well, Christy, we've got a problem here," he began to tell her. "You've got a growth on your cervix, and it's pretty angry-looking. It may very well be cancer."

He paused to let this thunderbolt have its effect. Christy was silent.

"We won't know for sure until we send some tissue to the lab and have one of the pathologists take a look at it. That should take a couple of days, so why don't we plan on seeing you again at the end of the week. Maybe Friday?" he asked.

Christy was still silent, shocked by this devastating news. *I've got to call Momma,* she thought.

"Christy, is Friday okay?" he repeated, not having received a response.

"Friday?" Christy echoed, trying to focus on what Dr. Simmons had just said. "Yes, Friday should be fine. And I'll bring my mother with me, if that's alright."

That had been six months ago.

"Christy, Mrs. McKenna, I think everything's in order," the hospice nurse told them. "Your pain medicine is right here, and if you need anything, just call me."

Polly McKenna, Christy's mother, walked the young nurse to the front door. It was already dark outside. Only six o' clock, but it was mid-January and the days were still short.

"Thanks, Jenny," she told the nurse. "Thanks for everything. You're so good with her."

"She's had a bad day today, hasn't she?" Jenny said.

"Yes, she has," Polly sighed. "And they seem to be getting worse, don't they?"

Jenny disappeared into the evening and Polly went back to her daughter's bedroom.

"Momma, you need to get some rest," Christy said, her voice a mere whisper now.

"Don't you worry about me," Polly said, making sure all of her daughter's medications were in order and easily accessible.

"You just haven't been sleeping much," Christy added. "And I don't want you to wear yourself out."

Polly looked down at her daughter. She was proud of the remarkable way Christy had handled the past few weeks. Her body had betrayed her, but her spirit had seemed to grow stronger with each passing day. Yet a bitter and unnamable fear was growing within Polly.

She had to look away from her daughter and busy herself. "Have you heard anything from Jane?" Polly asked her.

The turning aside of Christy's head was answer enough.

Jane was Christy's older sister. She lived in California with her husband, Jeremy, and their six-month-old son, Azure. The two sisters hadn't seen each other in more than five years, and they had only spoken once during that time. Even that one occasion had occurred by accident. It had been Christmas Eve and Jane had dialed her mother's house and Christy had picked up the phone.

"Let me speak to Mother," Jane had said.

The girls had been very close growing up, sharing clothes and friends, and occasionally boyfriends. Then Jane had gone to school in Los Angeles and met and fallen in love with a fellow student, Jeremy. He was a self-defined "free spirit," and when he had come to Rock

Hill to officially meet the folks and declare his intentions, there had been immediate friction. Polly and Mat McKenna had done the best they could to make him feel welcome and a part of the family, but there had been a growing rub.

It had all exploded one afternoon when Mat sat down with Jeremy and expressed his thoughts about marriage.

"Jeremy, I guess you know this is very important to us," he had told him. "I don't know about your religious convictions, but I think you know what Jane believes. She was raised in the Baptist church, and I assume she wants to be married here in Rock Hill."

Jeremy had sat quietly during this conversation, studying the backs of his hands.

"Our minister strongly recommends several premarital counseling sessions," Mat told him, "and he can meet with the two of you this Saturday, if that suits. He's a low-key guy and I think you'll like him."

Jeremy looked up and said, "Mr. McKenna, no offense, but I'm not into that stuff. I guess you would call me an agnostic, or maybe a universalist. Jane and I have agreed to disagree on that one. Anyway, we've decided to get married in California, at a friend's house that overlooks the ocean. It'll be a civil service, so I don't suppose we'll be needing to meet with your preacher."

That had started a widening rift. Mat and Polly had talked with their daughter and soon realized there was no common ground and no room for compromise. They were disappointed and concerned, but reluctant to be the ones to place a wedge between themselves and their daughter, who would be living a continent away.

Christy had not been as complacent and accepting. She and Jane had gotten into a bitter argument late one night, and hurtful things were said and cruel accusations made. In the end, Jane had felt she had to choose between Jeremy and her family, and she chose Jeremy. She faulted Christy for being what she saw as the "tip of the spear."

The couple had been married on a bluff overlooking the Pacific Ocean, with none of Jane's family members present.

"She hasn't called?" Polly persisted.

"No, she hasn't," Christy answered weakly.

"Well, maybe I'll—" Polly began but was interrupted.

"No, just leave it alone, Momma. She'll call when she's ready."

Polly wasn't sure about that. Jane was in some sort of denial and had been since the diagnosis of inoperable cervical cancer had been made. She and Mat had called her and tried to explain what was going on.

"Jane, your sister is very sick," they had told her. "Dr. Simmons performed a routine examination and found a tumor on her cervix. It turned out to be cancer, and a CT scan showed that it's spread through her abdomen and to her liver. He can't operate on it, so they'll be trying chemo and some other things. He said that if she had just had a Pap smear…"

Jane had been silent to that point and then she'd interrupted. "I had an abnormal Pap smear a few years ago, some inflammation or something like that. I just had to take some medicine and then it went away. Everything's fine now." And then she went still. That was all she said. No questions, no messages for Christy, nothing. And she hadn't called her sister in all these months.

This was a heartache that was hard for Polly and Mat to bear. They had called Jane on several other occasions, but the response was always the same. She didn't seem to be hearing them.

Polly kissed her daughter's forehead, told her goodnight, and quietly left the room. She made sure the night-light was on and the door was slightly cracked.

That night, they panicked. The people from hospice were wonderful, and they had clearly and accurately explained the dying process to Polly and Mat. The staff had been uncanny in their ability to map out these final few weeks and days, and had told them the end was fast approaching.

The McKennas thought they would be ready for this, but at midnight when Christy began making gurgling sounds and was no longer responsive, they panicked and called 9-1-1. Then Mat called Jane and told her Christy was dying.

I was in the ER when they came in. The paramedics took Christy to the Cardiac room and Jeff and I followed.

I had never seen Christy before, but it was obvious to me she was terminally ill. Her wasted frame caused me to look up at Denton, the lead paramedic, and start to ask a question.

His eyes and a nod of his head indicated I should look behind me. Mat and Polly McKenna had come into the room and were standing at the foot of the stretcher, their arms around each other. Polly was looking down at her daughter and was crying. Mat looked at me with reddened eyes and a hopeless and helpless look on his face.

They told me Christy's story, and I understood what needed to happen. She was near death, with agonal respirations and a slowing and weakening pulse. It would not be long. Once I was sure Mat and Polly understood what was happening and would be all right, Jeff and I left the room. The telemetry monitor at the nurses' station would tell me when it was over.

Jane had caught the first flight she could arrange out of Los Angeles, but there had been several delays. She made it to Rock Hill in time for the visitation and the funeral.

◈

Stewart Donaldson was on his way in again. Denton Roberts had just called in on the EMS radio and given us a report: chest pain, shortness of breath, low blood pressure. We had been here before.

Stewart was 61 years old and was a retired chemist. He and his wife, Maggie, lived in a small house on the outskirts of town where they had raised their three children and where she maintained one of the finest rose gardens in the county. Five or six years ago Stewart had suffered a heart attack, a massive one. He had barely made it to the ER. I had been on duty that night, and we had struggled to stabilize him and then get him to the cath lab. The cardiologist told him he had small-vessel disease and it was not amenable to bypass surgery. They had placed a couple of stents in his coronary arteries, and this had worked for about a year. Then he'd had another heart attack, not as bad as the first, but it had knocked off a little bit more of his heart muscle.

Stewart had tried everything: medications, diet, exercise. Nothing seemed to be working. He'd continued to have episodes of chest pain and then several additional small heart attacks. With each of them he lost a little more of his heart. The last time he had been in the ER he'd been in congestive heart failure, his diseased heart failing to pump out the blood that was returning to it. His lungs had filled with fluid and he had almost died. He had survived that episode but now he was on a precarious balance beam, with any new stress or new development threatening to tip him into failure again.

Stewart and Maggie had considered a heart transplant but had decided against it. The chance of his surviving the surgery was too small, and the aftermath was too frightening. And they weren't even sure they could get on a waiting list.

They had resolved to deal with his heart condition as best they could and accept what each day brought. Recently, not many of those days had been very good.

It was a little after three o'clock in the afternoon when Denton wheeled Stewart into the department. Stewart looked up and smiled at me as he passed the nurses' station. His color was bad, and he was struggling for breath. Maggie followed a few steps behind.

Lori was waiting for them in Cardiac and helped Denton transfer him to our stretcher.

"The last reading I got was 60 over 40," he told her. That was a dangerously low blood pressure and would limit some of the interventions we would be able to try.

Lori attached his electrodes to our heart monitor and waited for the screen to come alive. An irregular beep...beep-beep...indicated that he was in an unusual rhythm and that his heart rate was rapid, somewhere around 120. None of this was good.

I walked over to the side of his stretcher and said, "Stewart, I thought you were going to stay away from this place."

He looked up and smiled. "Well, Dr. Lesslie, I tried. But I suppose I just wanted to come and visit."

He had difficulty speaking, and this brief sentence tired him. I patted his shoulder, noting that his skin was cool and sweaty.

"That's okay," I told him. "We're always glad to see you and Maggie." She had come into the room with him and was standing behind me, making sure she was out of our way.

"Are you having any pain today?" I asked him.

He shook his head, conserving his energy.

"Just the shortness of breath?" I pursued.

This time he nodded and as he did so, the nasal prongs that were delivering oxygen slipped from his nose. Lori reached over and gently replaced them, tightening the straps that went over his ears.

After I examined Stewart I said, "We'll need to get a chest X-ray and EKG. And we'll need to check some labs to see just where we are. That shouldn't take long."

Turning to his wife I told her, "Maggie, you can stay in here with him if you want. We're going to try a few things to help his breathing, but you won't be in the way."

"Of course," she said. "And I'll just stay right over here." She patted the countertop behind her and stepped closer to it. "Oh, and Dr. Lesslie," she added. "I brought you something."

She had a rose in her hand, its stem wrapped in aluminum foil. It was a single dark red bloom, and it was beautiful.

"I was hoping you would be on duty today," she said, smiling. "I remember you liked the darker roses, and my Black Magic is just now blooming. Here, this is for you." She handed me the flower.

I vaguely remembered talking with her at some point in the past about her roses, and I must have expressed my preferences. Her memory impressed me.

"Maggie, you didn't have to do this," I said, taking the rose from her. "This is really thoughtful."

"Just be sure to put it in some water," she instructed me, wiping her hands together.

I took the rose and stepped out of the room just as the X-ray techs entered, rolling their portable machine.

Thirty minutes later we had enough information to know that Stewart had suffered another heart attack and was in worsening heart failure. He had responded a little to the oxygen and the small amount of medicine we could give him to reduce the fluid in his lungs. There just weren't many options for him at this point.

I had called his cardiologist and he had mentioned trying the things we had already done.

"Well, Robert," he had told me, "there's just not much else we can do for Mr. Donaldson. If you want me to put him in the hospital, I will. But it sounds like this is going to be the end for him."

This was blunt, but his words were true. This reality had been hovering around me, but I had been unwilling to grapple with it. Now I must.

"Thanks. I'll give you a call if something changes."

As I hung up the phone, Lori asked me, "Did he have anything to offer? Any ideas?"

"No, nothing," I said. "Just pretty much what we already know. Stewart's not doing well, and I don't know if he is going to survive the evening. I need to go talk with them."

One of our techs was adjusting Stewart's monitor as I entered the room.

"Sandy," I said to her. "I need to talk with the Donaldsons, if you wouldn't mind stepping out for a minute."

She finished adjusting the leads and checked the rate of the IV fluids. "Sure," she said. "I'll be right outside."

She closed the door behind her and I was alone with the couple.

Maggie was standing by the head of the stretcher and was gently stroking Stewart's hair. He was still struggling for breath, though not quite as badly now. He was able to talk but not in long stretches.

"Well, Doctor, what does it look like?" he asked.

I pulled a stool over and sat down by his side, his chart in my lap.

"Pretty much what we thought, Stewart," I said to him. "And probably what the two of you thought. It looks like you've had another heart attack and it's tipped you over into congestive failure."

"Hmm," he mused. "We've been here before." He paused and caught his breath. "But this seems a little worse somehow."

Maggie stopped caressing her husband's head and said, "Dr. Lesslie, how bad is it? What do you really think?"

I glanced over at his monitor and noted that his heart rate had slowed a little, but it continued to struggle along in the 110-to-120-per-minute range. Still not good.

Looking at Maggie and then at Stewart, I told them, "You know, how bad it is really doesn't matter. Your blood work shows you've had more heart muscle damage, and we all know you didn't have much if any to spare. Any further heart tissue loss would be...would put you—"

"Am I going to die?" Stewart asked straight up. He was calm as he said this, and Maggie didn't flinch. I knew I needed to be honest with them and tell them what I thought and felt.

Still, it was difficult. I cleared my voice before beginning.

"Stewart, I don't think your heart can take much more. We've run out of options here to help you, and I...I think it's just a matter of time. Maybe not much time."

He didn't say anything but just raised his left hand in the air and Maggie reached down and grasped it. She was nodding her head and I saw that her eyes glistened, but there were no tears.

"Okay," he said with a new and surprising firmness in his voice. "Where do we go from here? We really don't want to be admitted to the hospital."

While he was catching his breath Maggie said, "How much time do you think we have? A day? Maybe two?"

I shook my head and said, "No, not a day. Maybe a few hours, or even less." It was difficult to say these words, but it was true. And they needed to know.

When she heard this, she took her husband's hand in both of hers and they looked at each other. He slowly nodded his head, wordlessly telling her that I was right.

For a moment the three of us remained silent. Then I stood up and walked to the edge of the bed.

"Let's do this," I began. "Stewart, I'm going to keep you here in the department for as long as I can. No, I'll keep you here in the department, period. And Maggie, you stay here with him. I'm going to have a more comfortable chair brought in for you, and if you need anything else, we'll be right outside the door. No one will bother you."

They looked at each other again and then at me.

Maggie spoke. "Thank you, Dr. Lesslie. We appreciate…" Her voice cracked, and I knew I had to leave the room. I turned away and walked to the door.

"Thank you, Dr. Lesslie," she said again.

Stewart and Maggie spent the next hour and twenty minutes together, talking and holding hands. They said the things they needed and wanted to say to each other, and then as Stewart's breathing became more labored, they fell silent.

Shortly after that, his monitor fell silent and Stewart was gone.

Later, after Maggie had gone home and the department had shifted into its usual evening rush of activity, I found myself walking up the hallway with three clipboards under my arms. There were new auto-accident victims in minor trauma, nothing serious, just a few bumps and bruises. As I neared the nurses' station, a flash of color caught my eye and I stopped.

On the countertop was Maggie's rose.

13

You're on My Last **Nerve**

*A man's wisdom gives him patience; it is to
his glory to overlook an offense.*

—Proverbs 19:11

In the ER, if you have not mastered the skill of patience, you subject
yourself to the risk of making unnecessary mistakes, distressing and
disappointing those who look to you as a leader, and feeling pretty
crummy at the end of your shift.

You feel crummy because some person or some situation has gotten
the better of you. In the ER we are frequently tested in this area,
and the testing usually comes in the form of an ER abuser. We need
to make the distinction here between an "ER regular" and an "ER
abuser." You have already met some of our "regulars," such as Slim
Brantley. Slim means no harm and his ultimate motivation for coming
to the ER is for food, warmth, and companionship.

An abuser, on the other hand, is frequently driven by sinister
purposes. These purposes usually involve obtaining an injection of
a potent pain medication, or even more desirable, the writing of a
prescription for the same. The realization of these goals is achieved
through deceit, deception, and sometimes violence.

Dealing with these individuals requires a large measure of patience
and a diminished view of the importance of "self." These interactions
are not contests between the ER doctor and a drug seeker. There is no
moral or righteous high ground on which to plant our banner. There
are no winners here—only the potential for all involved to be losers.

This was a difficult lesson for me to learn. I was amazed, as an intern, by the tenacity of these individuals, and by their audacity. My hackles went up when a "seeker" presented himself or herself to the department, and I believed it was my sworn and sacred duty to uncover and thwart their crafty and cunning efforts. I would not be bested.

⸎

11:55 p.m. I was at the nurses' station, contemplating the stack of charts of patients who were awaiting my attention. The double-cover doctor had left at eleven, leaving me with five or six people to take care of. Thankfully they all had seemingly trivial problems.

"Why don't you get this place cleaned out," Trish, our unit secretary said to me. She smiled, leaned back in her chair, and put her hands behind her head. "One of the nurses from 3North is going out for pizza and said she'll pick us up something if we want."

I was finishing up the record of a kid with strep throat and glanced again at the unseen stack of charts.

"Shouldn't take too long," I answered, unbothered by her gentle chiding. "Why don't you go ahead and get something organized. See what everyone wants."

After placing the kid's chart in the discharge rack, I picked up the record of the next patient to be seen. Room 3A: "Cough and can't sleep."

As I turned toward the door of room 3, my attention was drawn to the triage entrance. Jeff was leading a young man into the department. He was making a note on the patient's chart, and when he briefly looked up, his eyes caught mine. He lowered his head just a little and raised his eyebrows. This signal, unseen by the patient behind him, told me something was up.

The twentysomething man was dressed in jeans and a T-shirt that advertised "MYRTLE BEACH." His flip-flops slapped the tiled floor as he was led to room 4. Under his arm he carried a smudged and worn X-ray folder.

I turned toward my coughing and sleep-deprived patient. I was curious about our new visitor in room 4, but he would have to wait his turn.

It was almost 1:30 in the morning, and the stack of charts on the counter had been reduced to just one, that of the patient in room 4. I had not had a chance to talk with Jeff about this guy, and right now Jeff was back out in triage.

I picked up the chart and looked at the chief complaint. "Right leg pain. History of bone cancer."

Hmm. That was a little unusual.

His vital signs were normal. No fever and no elevated heart rate. A rapid heartbeat can be a reasonably good indicator of significant pain and stress. There was nothing else on the chart of any particular interest, except that he listed a city in Florida as his residence. Then I noticed that the ER business office had handwritten "No picture ID" on the bottom of his personal information sheet. This was beginning to smell a little peculiar, and instinctively my defenses were on alert.

Pulling the curtain aside, I stepped into his room. John Glover was sitting on the stretcher, his legs dangling over the side. He looked up as I entered and immediately began rubbing his right thigh.

"Hey, Doc. I hope you can help me," he implored.

I stepped across the room and sat down in the chair opposite his stretcher.

"I'm Dr. Lesslie," I introduced myself. "What can we do for you tonight?"

He continued to rub his thigh and looked down at this apparently painful appendage. "It's this leg, Doc. About eight months ago I started having some pain right here," he began, pointing to the mid-front of his thigh. "Not bad at first, but it just kept on hurting. After a few weeks I couldn't stand it any longer and I went to see a doctor."

At this point he stopped rubbing his thigh long enough to pat the X-ray folder lying beside him on the stretcher. "They got some X-rays and gave me some awful news. I've got bone cancer, and they say it's pretty bad."

He put his head in his hands and shook it from side to side. I was impressed.

"I'm on my way to see my sister in Virginia and I ran out of pain medicine. I just need enough for about two weeks. And if I make it that long, I'll be back home in Florida and can see my own doctor."

I was about to ask something when he spoke again. "Oh, and when it gets this bad, they usually give me a shot of Demerol and either Tylox or Percocet. That's what usually helps."

He looked at me expectantly and added, "Sometimes Oxycontin works the best."

Oftentimes I wonder just what people are thinking, and what they take us for. Do they think we wouldn't notice such a flagrantly inappropriate appeal? Or that we would immediately head for the drug cabinet and give them whatever they want? This guy obviously needed help, but it would be of a psychological nature, not physical. However, I knew he wouldn't be interested in anything at this point other than procuring narcotics. And in the ER, it was almost impossible to provide the sort of assistance he ultimately needed. My job was to sniff him out as a drug abuser, frustrate his perfidious efforts, and send him on his way.

I was up to the task, and I knew it.

"Well, we'll see what we can do to help," I assured him, considering my best course of action here. "Can I take a look at your X-rays?" I asked.

"Sure, Doc, help yourself," he answered, handing me the folder. "But could you please hurry? My leg is killing me."

"I'll be right back," I replied, and stepped out of the room.

Jeff was pushing a wheelchair into the department from triage, laden with a middle-aged man. This latest patient was having trouble breathing and was obviously struggling.

"Shortness of breath and a history of emphysema," Jeff informed me. "I'm taking him to room 6."

I knew it would take a few minutes for Jeff to get him on the stretcher and get things started. I would have enough time to look at Mr. Glover's X-rays.

"I'll be right there," I told Jeff. "Holler out if you need me."

I walked over to the X-ray viewing box, took out the two X-rays in the folder, and snapped them into the holders at the top of the box. I stepped back and looked at the films. The first thing I noticed was the top right corner, the area where the patient's ID information was usually included, had been cut away. Both X-rays were missing this same irregular rectangle. There was no way to identify the person whose images were before me on the screen. And then I noticed that at the bottom right-hand corner, completely contrary to any notational convention of which I was aware, someone had handwritten "John Glover" in black felt pen. No date. No identifying hospital. Hmm.

The X-rays were indeed of someone's femur. And that person, whoever and wherever they might be, was certainly unfortunate. The X-rays revealed a large bone cancer sitting squarely in the middle of his or her thigh. But it was impossible to know when these films had been made, or where. What was possible to know was that this person had either lost his leg or his life. This was a bad-looking tumor.

Where had John Glover gotten these X-rays? Was it someone he knew, maybe a family member? Did he have access to some Radiology department somewhere? My curiosity was morphing into anger as I realized the depth to which this young man had sunk in order to satisfy his need for drugs. Whether he was using them himself or selling them made no difference. Then I remembered the patient Jeff had just taken to room 6, and I knew I would soon be needed. I left the X-rays hanging on the view box and walked across the department.

It took about 45 minutes to get our patient with shortness of breath under better control. He had developed pneumonia, superimposed on poor lung function induced by 35 years of work in a cotton mill. He was in less distress now, but he was still sick and would have to be admitted to the hospital.

Stepping out of room 6, I walked to the nurses' station and remembered the X-rays John Glover had brought with him. I glanced over at the view box where I had left them. They were gone. The curtain of room 4 was drawn closed, so I assumed Mr. Glover was still there.

"Trish, did you see what happened to the X-rays I was looking at a little while ago?" I asked, motioning with my head toward the view box.

"Yeah," she answered, not looking up from the work she was doing. "The guy in room 4 came out and went over and got them. He stuck 'em back in his folder and went back to his room. He wanted to know how much longer it was going to be."

As I stood at the nurses' station I could hear Jeff's deep, reassuring voice coming from behind the curtain of room 6.

"You're going to be alright, Mr. Jones," he was saying. "You're breathing easier now, and we're going to be able to treat your pneumonia. You're going to be okay."

I couldn't make out Mr. Jones's response. But the thought suddenly struck me—here was a man who was struggling for his life. He had come to us for help, and we were giving him just that. We were doing what we were trained to do, and were doing it effectively. This is why we were in the ER at one o'clock in the morning.

Then I glanced at the curtain of room 4 and felt my face flush a little. This John Glover, or whoever he was, had no reason to be in this department. He was taking up our space and our time. I picked up his chart and walked across to his room.

For a passing moment, I considered flushing him out. I would go into the room and tell him that I had reviewed his X-rays and that he indeed had a very serious case of bone cancer. I would tell him I knew it must be very painful, but just to be sure where we stood, I was going to send him around to the Radiology Department for some current films. We would know more about the status of his cancer and be able to more effectively treat him. Then I would watch him squirm.

The moment passed, as did the temptation. As satisfying as that might be for me, I knew what I must do.

I pulled the curtain aside, and seemingly on cue he began rubbing his leg again.

"They haven't brought me anything for pain yet, Doc. Any idea when that's going to happen?" he asked. "This leg is killing me, and I really need to get on the road."

I clutched his chart to my chest and lowered my head, fixing my eyes on his.

"Mr. Glover, I think we both know what's going on here," I began. "Those are not your X-rays and you don't have bone cancer."

He immediately stopped rubbing his thigh, and his head tilted ever so slightly to one side. He continued to stare at me.

"You're not going to receive any pain medication here, or any prescriptions. You've taken up enough of our time, and I would suggest you leave this ER."

I stopped and waited for a response. For a moment he was silent, and he just stared at me. Then very calmly, he picked up the X-ray folder and stood up.

"Doc, you can just kiss my butt."

His shoulder brushed mine as he walked out of the room. I felt my face flush again, and I followed him as he walked toward the exit. I wanted to say something, something that would cut him to the quick, but I thought better of it. I was trying to regain control of myself and of this situation.

And then I remembered the X-ray folder. The doors to the exit had just closed and I hurriedly stepped toward them. What was I thinking? I needed to get those X-rays and destroy them. John Glover, probably using another name, would soon be in another ER, rubbing the same leg, asking for the same medicine, and exhibiting the same X-rays. Maybe even later this very night.

I was going to get those X-rays from him. That was the least I could do.

Stepping out into the ambulance area, I could just make out his shadow, retreating into the parking lot. There was no one else in sight.

"John," I called out to him. "Hold on just a minute."

I quickened my pace, determined that he not leave until I had what I wanted.

He stopped at the top of a small rise, silhouetted against the glare of a lamp post at the back of the large lot. Turning, he faced me, just forty or fifty feet distant.

"Hold up," I called. And then he did something that made me stop in my tracks. He was carrying the folder in his right hand, and slowly he transferred it to his left. Then, nonchalantly but with obvious purpose, he shoved his right hand into his pants pocket and withdrew something. It wasn't large enough to be a gun, but the fleeting glint of reflected metal registered somewhere in my brain. What was I doing?

He didn't step toward me, just stood there, waiting. Silent.

I remained there for a moment, torn between walking up the hill and confronting him and simply turning and walking away. I looked at his right hand and tried to discern what object might be hidden there. He wasn't that big a guy. How dangerous could he be? All I was interested in was getting those X-rays, nothing more. I wasn't looking for a physical confrontation, and I would bet he wasn't either.

Wait a minute! What was I thinking? There was no dilemma here.

I turned and walked back to the ER.

Once again at the nurses' station, I addressed Trish. "You might want to give a few of the surrounding ERs a heads-up on Mr. Glover. Let them know his age and that he's got some X-rays with him of someone with bone cancer. Drug seeker, and maybe dangerous. They can call me if they have any questions."

I had a few minutes to reflect upon this encounter. I began to realize how foolish my behavior had been, and that I had let my emotions cloud my judgment. This had been a potentially dangerous situation and I had put myself in harm's way. And for what? To prove to this man that I had sniffed him out as a drug seeker? That this was my ER and he was not going to walk in and make demands of us? That we were no local yokels, easily deceived and manipulated?

It was an issue of pride. I would have to overcome this and learn to be patient in these circumstances. I would need to learn to be more objective and more pragmatic. I would need to learn to control whatever it was that drove me to seek dominance in such a situation.

I was learning. But I wasn't there yet. Another lesson awaited me, and this would be one of those rare times when I would be able to gain some valuable insight from the misstep of another.

6:30 P.M. It was a busy Saturday evening. I was working with one of our young partners, Andy James. He had finished his residency training a few months earlier, and was bright, eager, and obsessive to an almost bothersome degree. He had come to us with a few rough spots, but we were all of the opinion these would soon enough be smoothed out. The ER of Rock Hill General had a way of doing that.

He was showing me the chest X-ray of a patient in room 5, asking for my opinion.

"Dr. Lesslie, does this look more like pneumonia or heart failure?" he queried, closely scrutinizing the films of this sixty-year-old man.

"First, Andy," I responded, "I want you to call me Robert, not Dr. Lesslie. Okay?"

I had requested this of him at least a dozen times since his arrival, and after each such request he would try to make the attempt at less formality. Eventually, he slid back into using this appellation, a remnant of his still-fresh residency training.

"Okay, Dr...I mean, Robert. What do you think?"

We were discussing the sometimes difficult distinction between these two different problems, when we both were distracted by the squawking of the EMS radio.

"General, this is Medic 3," the familiar voice of one of our paramedics announced.

Lori walked over to the phone and pushed the hands-free button, allowing her to speak to the paramedic and for us to hear what was going on. Andy immediately walked over to the counter of the nurses' station and leaned closer to the phone.

"Go ahead, Medic 3. This is the General ER," Lori responded, taking out her pen and preparing to make some notes. She glanced at the clock on the wall and jotted down the time.

The paramedic proceeded to tell us that he was in transit with three patients from a motor-vehicle accident. And that Medic 4 would be bringing in another three from the same accident.

Andy's eyes widened. He looked in my direction.

"Nothing serious," the paramedic announced. "Neck and back pain. We have a few of them in full spinal protocol."

"10-4," Lori responded. "Minor trauma on arrival."

"10-4 to that," the paramedic answered. "Medic 3 out."

Andy had been making some notes as well.

"Sounds like it could be something bad," he said to me. "That's a lot of PIs (personal injuries) in one accident."

"We'll see," I answered, not yet impressed. Putting three patients in one ambulance was an indication the paramedics working the accident were not too concerned with the possibility of significant injury. And then there was the relaxed tone of the paramedic's voice.

"We'll see," I repeated.

Twenty minutes later, six young men from the auto accident were crowded into our minor trauma room. Three were on backboards, their heads securely taped in a rigid position. They had complained of neck pain, and the EMS squads were taking no chances. The other three victims were casually sitting in chairs, rubbing various body parts.

As Andy and I walked into the room one of the paramedics pulled me aside.

"Doc, somethin' suspicious is going on here," he told me. "This was a one-car accident, in the middle of town. Couldn't have been going more than 25 miles an hour, and there's no obvious damage to the car." He scratched his head and surveyed the congested room. "Good luck with these guys."

"Thanks," I said, noticing that Andy was in the far corner, questioning and examining one of the patients who had been secured on one of the backboards.

"Where exactly do you hurt?" I heard him ask.

Lori came up behind me and tapped me on the shoulder. "Dr. Lesslie, I've got a seventy-five-year-old in Cardiac with chest pain and a blood pressure of 60."

I glanced once more at the confusion in minor trauma. No one seemed to be seriously hurt, and Andy should be able to handle this. Anyway, I was needed up front.

"I'm right behind you," I said to Lori as we headed up the hall.

Two hours and a bunch of X-rays later, Andy had managed to clear all six patients involved in the auto accident. Everyone had checked out okay. No one had any obvious injury, and all the X-rays were normal. He stood beside me at the nurses' station, writing up the charts of these patients.

"I think they're going to be okay," he told me. "I didn't detect any significant neurological injuries."

"Well, that's a good thing," I responded, suppressing a smile. We had known that from the first moment, "we" meaning everyone other than Andy. But something still wasn't right here. Things didn't quite add up. I had been too busy to try to sort this out, but that moment of clarity was fast approaching.

We were still standing at the counter, when a police officer walked up. He was accompanied by a diminutive, bespectacled forty-year-old man. He shuffled along with the officer, looking down at the floor.

"Doc," the officer said. "I need to talk to you about the auto accident downtown, and about those guys involved. Mr. Grant here has some interesting information for you."

Andy immediately stopped what he was doing, looked up at the officer, and edged closer to where we were standing.

"What's going on here, Mr. Grant?" I asked him. "Do you have something to tell us?"

Mr. Grant fidgeted and put his hands in his pockets. Reluctantly, he looked up at me.

"I don't want to get into any trouble," he began. "And I don't want anyone else to get into trouble," he continued, nervously looking down the hallway. "But there's something you need to know."

The police officer was silently nodding his head.

"That accident, the one with all those people…" he began. "It didn't exactly happen the way they said it did."

I glanced at Andy. He had a troubled look on his face.

"What exactly do you mean?" I asked him.

"Well, I know they told you they ran into a telephone pole, and they were all thrown around inside the car and everything. And they told you that two of them had been crossing the street when the car knocked 'em down. That's how they said they got hurt."

"You're right, Mr. Grant. That's what they told us," Andy excitedly interjected. "They all told us the same story."

Mr. Grant looked in his direction and then back at me.

"Well," he started again. "I was there, and I saw what happened."

"You were in the accident?" I asked him. "You were in the car?"

"No, no. I was walking down the sidewalk when it happened. I saw the whole thing."

The police officer was nodding his head again, and smiling.

"Yeah, I saw the whole thing," our volunteer witness continued. "It was like in slow motion. I was walking down the street, and then here comes this car, headed straight for the curb. The driver wasn't paying attention and the car clipped a couple of parked vehicles and then came to a stop. Barely bumped those cars," he added, shaking his head. "But the main thing is there were only two guys in the car. The driver and a front-seat passenger. That was it."

"Wait a minute," Andy said, becoming a little agitated. "There were six people in the accident. You can go back there and count them."

"I know what they told you," Mr. Grant responded. "But there were only two people in that car. The other four were standing on the sidewalk when it happened. They must have known the driver of the car, 'cause as soon as it happened, two of them ran over and piled in. And the other two just sorta looked around and then fell down on the ground, right in front of the car. Then they all started rubbin' their necks and rolling around."

"You're kidding," I said, amused by their audacity.

"They did what?" Andy asked angrily. "You mean these guys weren't even in the accident? They're committing fraud?"

"That's exactly right," Mr. Grant said. "Nobody was hurt in that fender bender, and it's all a hoax. That's why I came down here. And that's why I found this officer and told him the story." He stood a little straighter now, and a little taller, having told us the truth and assisted in the now-inevitable triumph of justice.

There was a moment of silence as this new revelation registered, and then I addressed the police officer. "What do you plan to do here?" I asked.

"Have you people medically cleared them?" he responded. "Are they free to go?"

"Yes," Andy said. "They're medically cleared and ready to be released. You're going to arrest them, aren't you?" he asked. "I mean, this must be some sort of a crime, isn't it?"

"Sure, there's misrepresentation and all of that. And probably some sort of fraud issues, I suppose," the officer said. "I dare say the insurance people will be interested in this, and I can assure you we're going to have a word of prayer with them down at the station."

"You mean this was all about collecting insurance money?" Andy asked, incredulous. "They've wasted our time—and the EMS call… What if someone had truly needed an ambulance and none was available because they were responding to this bogus accident?"

I was going to try to calm Andy, but when I turned to face him, he had already headed off down the hall toward minor trauma.

"Uh-oh," I said, and followed him. The officer was right behind me.

Andy stood in the doorway of the crowded room with his hands on his hips and began to harangue the miscreants. Freed from their backboards, they were all huddled in the back left corner of the room, either sitting or standing.

"What were you people thinking?" he began. He then lined out their multiple crimes against humanity and the great risk they had imposed upon the people of this community. He dwelt at length on the possibility of truly needy patients not being able to receive care from the EMS system because they had been inappropriately tied up.

Amazingly, the six gentlemen stayed where they were and calmly took this diatribe. To be sure, there was open hostility on the faces of a few of them, and one or two stared blankly at the ceiling. Then I looked behind me and understood the reason for their acquiescence. The police officer was standing behind us, a good head-and-a-half taller than Andy. The look on his face clearly commanded their silence.

Andy finished, his face red with righteous indignation. Then he turned and walked past us. He didn't notice the wink the officer gave me.

I understood the anger Andy felt in this situation. Blatant abuse is hard to deal with, under any circumstance. But in this instance I was able to be a spectator, and I was able to analyze what had happened here over the past few hours. Andy was justified in his indignation, but what had this confrontation accomplished? Andy might have felt some sense of relief, having blown off some steam and calling these guys out, but I doubt it. He would still be stewing about this when he drove home at seven in the morning. And the six perpetrators? They had no sense of wrongdoing. Their concern now was the immediate repercussions of their actions, nothing more. Their core values had not been altered by Andy's admonitions.

So everyone here had really been a loser. Wait—there was the police officer. He might be the only winner. He had gotten a little chuckle out of the happenings in minor trauma.

I was going to remember this.

You have to have a lot of patience to learn patience.

—Stanislaw Lec (1909–1966)

14

On **Crossing** the **Bar**

When the perishable has been clothed with the imperishable,
and the mortal with immortality, then the saying that is writ-
ten will come true: "Death has been swallowed up in victory."

—1 Corinthians 15:54-55

For those of us in the ER, dealing with death in our own depart-ment is difficult enough. But from time to time we are also called upon to deal with a death that has occurred elsewhere in the hospital. When someone dies, a physician is needed to certify and then docu-ment that a death has actually occurred. This responsibility clearly falls to the treating physician. However, if it's late at night or the middle of a weekend and that patient's physician is not in the hospital, the ER doc on duty might seem a reasonable alternative. After all, he or she is in the hospital, awake, and "available."

Pronouncing the death of a patient is something we had performed in the past as a courtesy extended to the medical staff. However, as the medical staff and hospital census grew, this practice became onerous for the ER physicians.

It isn't only that we are pulled out of the department at inopportune times. After all we don't lock the doors to the ER while we are gone, and patients don't stop coming in. Imagine the response if we called the involved physician when we returned to the department and asked him to come in and help because we had gotten backed up.

The real objection we have is that on occasion we go upstairs to find the recently deceased surrounded by a room full of family members.

These people are complete strangers to us and they are understandably upset and distraught.

And then come the questions:

"Who are you?"

"Where is his doctor?"

"What caused her to die?"

"Do you think he suffered?"

"What do we do now?"

These are all things we are, in most cases, unprepared to answer. (I can usually handle the first one.) It is always an awkward moment for the family and for us. Our current policy is that we will go upstairs when practicable, document the person's death, and then note the time on the death certificate and in the patient's chart. This should only take a few minutes, and then we are able to return to the ER. It is the responsibility of the patient's physician, coordinating with the unit charge nurse, to be sure the family has been notified and left the patient's room. This is not a perfect solution, but it is a reasonable compromise.

In the past, there were a few members of the medical staff in particular who seemed to always forget the part about taking care of the family. And there we would be, opening the door and being confronted by grieving strangers.

Dr. Bill Jones, whose patient I was to deal with very early one morning, did not fall into this group. He was appreciative of our help and always made that clear. He understood the position we were in, and the potential dilemma. Still, it was a hassle.

Yet isn't it interesting that something you view as a hassle, something that is a real nuisance or inconvenience, can actually become a profound and meaningful experience? These things happen when we least expect them. They present themselves at unusual times and places. I think you need to be at least a little receptive to such a possibility—or the opportunity passes, forever lost. I wonder how many of these opportunities I have missed.

❧

Bill Jones had called and asked me to go upstairs and pronounce one of his patients.

"Sure, Bill," I responded. "Mr. Blake in 432?" I confirmed, making a note on a scrap of paper.

"Yes, that's right," he answered. "Eighty-two years old, I think. Cancer of the pancreas. The family has already gone home. They were expecting this, and I'll talk with them in the morning."

"Okay, I'll take care of it," I told him, and handed the phone back to the unit secretary.

I took a look around the department, and stepped out into the triage area. Jeff was on duty here and was standing at the reception desk, talking to the third-shift secretary and our security guard for the evening. The waiting room was empty.

"Looks pretty quiet?" I observed.

He turned to me and said, "Yeah, knock on wood. We're under control."

"Good," I said. "I've got to go upstairs and pronounce a patient for Dr. Jones. Up on 4East. If you need me, just have the operator page. But I should only be a couple of minutes."

"Will do," he answered, then returned to his conversation.

The elevator ascended smoothly, and for a moment I was alone with my thoughts. *How many times have I done this? Too many.* And I suspect there will be many more. It is a perfunctory task. Check for a pulse. Check for any respirations. Note the time on the chart. Almost always, these are people I don't know and have never seen. Sometimes I will find myself pronouncing a patient I had seen in the ER a few days earlier and who had then been admitted to the hospital for a serious problem. Occasionally it would be someone I had seen and who had then been admitted with what seemed to be a routine and non-life-threatening condition. Those deaths surprised me. They were unexpected, and I would wonder what might have gone wrong.

And rarely it would be a friend or acquaintance of mine—usually an elderly individual whose presence in the hospital caught me unaware. These are always somber times for me, and the only occasions when I don't mind family members being present.

The doors of the elevator opened slowly and I stepped onto the fourth floor, facing the nursing station. The upper floors of the hospital were designed as a large "wheel," with the nursing area in the center and four "spokes" extending outward. These "spokes" contained the patient rooms, and were designated North, East, South, and West. I stepped over to the central counter, a circular structure where one of the unit nurses was sitting and writing on a chart. She looked up as I walked over.

"Good morning, Dr. Lesslie," she welcomed me, smiling.

I looked at the clock on the wall behind her. *2:35 a.m.* It didn't feel like it, but I guess in fact it *was* morning.

"I suppose you're here for Mr. Blake in 432." She closed the chart she had been writing in and handed it to me.

"Yeah, that's Dr. Jones's patient, right?" I asked, taking the chart. Reflexively, I checked the room number and patient name on the top of the clipboard. "432—Blake." Just wanted to be sure. On more than one occasion I had been handed the wrong patient chart and had walked into a room with family members present and proceeded to look pretty goofy. I never wanted that to happen again.

"That's right. We checked on him a little while ago, and he had passed," she confirmed. "He was a real nice man," she added.

"Thanks," I tucked his chart under my arm and walked toward the east spoke of the wheel.

The even-numbered rooms were on the right side of the hallway, and 432 was about halfway down the hall. The door was partly open and I stepped through, pulling it closed behind me.

The room was dark, illuminated only by the pale fluorescent glow of a small fixture over the head of the bed and the faint light of a new moon as it shone through the open window. It took a moment for my eyes to adjust to the change.

I walked over to the edge of the bed and looked down. Mr. Blake lay peacefully, covered with a blanket that had been tucked neatly under his chin. His head rested on a pillow, his eyes were closed, and his mouth was partly open. I watched him for a minute and could not discern any respirations. I put my stethoscope in my ears and, pulling the blanket down, exposed his chest. I checked for any cardiac activity or movement of air. None. After carefully replacing his blanket I opened his medical chart, found the appropriate page, and struggled in the faint light to make a few notes. "No respirations. No cardiac activity. Pronounced dead at 2:27 a.m."

That was it. I had officially documented the death of this complete stranger. He had been born eighty-some years ago, and now he was gone. I stepped back from the bed and found the scene strangely peaceful. It was completely quiet, and the moon shining through the window added a surreal touch. Then it occurred to me that I was an interloper. This was a profound moment, the ending of a man's life. And though I was on official business, I was in fact a stranger.

I turned to the door and jumped, when from the far corner of the room I heard a man's voice. "He's at peace now."

Stopping in my tracks, I stared in the direction of this voice and tried to determine its source. In the shadowed right-hand corner of the room, I began to make out the form of a man sitting in a chair. He shifted in his seat, clearly declaring his presence.

"Yes, he is," I answered. "I'm Dr. Lesslie. And you are…?"

"I'm his son, Paul Blake," came the response.

We were silent for a moment. Strangely this unexpected interruption didn't bother me, though now even more than before it occurred to me that I indeed was interrupting this scene.

"Yeah, he's at peace now," Paul repeated. "It's been a tough couple of weeks. Cancer of the pancreas is a…" He paused, searching for the words that could somehow sum up his father's last weeks of pain and suffering. There were no adequate words for this, nor for the loss that Paul had anticipated and that was now crushing him. "He suffered a good bit the last few days. But last night he was real calm, and we talked for a good bit. And his pain seemed to be better."

Paul Blake shifted again in his chair. "At about midnight, Rachel—that's his wife, my momma—told him it was time and it was all right to let go."

He paused and collected himself. "And that seemed to release him. He got real quiet and peaceful. And in a little while, he just stopped breathing."

He was silent, and I wasn't sure I needed to respond. But somehow this was an unusual moment and I was led to say, "You know, sometimes that's what it takes. When nothing else can be done, it's the words of a wife, or husband, or some other loved one that can make the difference. And you're right about 'release.' Sometimes that's what has needed to happen. And it takes a strong person to be able to release a loved one."

"You're right," he answered. "Momma was a strong person. And right now, I miss her something awful. She's been dead five years."

What had I just heard? I looked around the room to be sure no one else was present. His mother was dead? And then I understood.

"Your daddy thought he was talking with his wife?"

"No. He didn't *think* he was talking with her. He knew he was. He was sort of muttering to himself, when he just stopped and looked straight at me. And then he was as clear as a bell. He told me what she'd said, and that it was going to be all right. And he told me he loved me. Then he was quiet. And that was it." Paul's voice was shaking at the end.

We were again silent. It was time for me to leave, and I cleared my throat and began to turn toward the door.

"That's why I'm sitting here, Doc." His voice pierced the shadows. "I'm waiting. I want to talk to my momma. I'm hoping she will say something to me, just like she did to Daddy."

I peered into the corner, trying to make out the face of this man. And then I looked again at his father, lying on the hospital bed. I put Mr. Blake's chart on the bedside table, pulled up the remaining chair in the room, and sat down.

Leaning forward with my elbows on my knees, I said, "Paul, I think I know how you feel."

"You do?" he asked. "I was about to give up and go home. But somehow, I just kept hoping. It seems like she's just so close right now."

"She is," I answered. "I don't know how, but I know she's right here. And she's with your daddy."

I could see his head nodding. "I know. But I just need something I can see, or feel. Something I can hear, so I can be sure. You know what I mean?"

"Yes. I know what you mean," I answered, knowing painfully too well.

"I know that Momma loved the Lord, and so did Daddy. And I know where they are right now. But it's awful lonely right here in this room. I'm not ready to lose them both. I'm not ready to be alone, without them."

I did know how that felt. My mother had died when I was fourteen, and my father had died several years ago. In a very real way, Paul and I were orphans. Our parents are no longer here to counsel us, to hold us, to give us advice. It's part of the cycle of life, but it's a painful part.

"Paul, I know we don't know each other, but let me share something with you."

I could see him settling back in his chair, his hands grasping the arm rests, his legs extended in front of him, crossed.

"As a physician, I'm trained to approach things from a scientific viewpoint. You stake out a theory and then you try to prove it. And if you can't prove it, if the evidence is not there, then you discard the idea and move on to another one. Now, scientific evidence is something we can see or feel. It's something that can be reproduced over and over again. If something is true here in Rock Hill, really true, then you should be able to observe the same thing, the same findings, in Chicago, in London, and in Australia. If you can't, then you're probably barking up the wrong tree."

I paused for a moment.

"Yeah, I understand that, Doc," Paul said.

"Well," I continued. "I have come to understand that there are things in this world, in this life, that don't fit that model. There are things that happen, things that are absolutely real that you can't put in a test tube, or see, or feel with your hands. But you know they are real, and they are true. Like your mother tonight, communicating with your daddy. I believe that is real. I don't think it was some semiconscious thought or some long-ago memory being awakened. I believe it happened."

Paul interrupted me. "Doc, I want to believe that too, and I think I do. But why can't I experience it? Why can't I talk with Momma just like Daddy did? I've been sitting, and waiting, and praying. And nothing. Just me in this room, alone, until you came in."

I leaned back in my chair now and looked out the window. The sliver of moon was now partially obscured by some quickly passing clouds, and the room had become darker.

"I understand what you're feeling," I told him. "But somehow, things don't work that way. There are definite moments of communication, of a sense of the real presence of a loved one, but they come at times of their own choosing. We can't command them or force them to occur. And I think it happens when it's supposed to happen. I think for a lot of us, it happens and we don't expect it, we don't understand it, and we don't accept it. You've seen it here tonight, with your father. And you know that it was real and you accept it as being real."

We were again silent, and I contemplated whether I should continue.

Paul gave me my answer. "You said you wanted to share something, Doc. What was that?"

It occurred to me that I was sharing some of my deepest thoughts and feelings with a complete stranger, in a darkened hospital room, in the middle of the night. Yet it was the right thing to do, the right moment.

"I told you my father died several years ago. He was in his mid seventies when that happened. He was an organic chemist, a professor, and the smartest man I have ever known. He had a lot of interests, but one of his passions was birds. He wouldn't allow any cats around the place, because they would bother the birds and drive them away. And his favorite was always the bluebird. I'm not sure why. Maybe their color, or their personality. But whatever the reason, wherever he lived he would build houses and feeders and work hard to attract bluebirds. And he was always successful. When I would visit and we would walk through the yard and talk, he would never fail to point out a particular birdhouse and describe 'the bluebird family' that lived there. I never quite understood his fascination with these birds, but I accepted it as part of who he was.

"He's buried about twenty minutes from here, in the cemetery behind the Neely's Creek ARP church. My mother is buried there too. About a year after Daddy died, I found myself on a highway not too far from the church. I had some time, so I drove over to the cemetery. It was a weekday afternoon and no one was around. It's a beautiful old cemetery, wide open, with a large magnolia near the place my parents are buried. I walked over to their graves and just stood there for several minutes. I read their headstones and it struck me that our lives, it seemed, could be summarized in just a few words and a few dates. But of course that's not true. These were my parents, and a life-time of memories came to my mind. They were good memories, and yet after a while, they became sad and painful. And I found myself feeling just like you described. I was without parents in this world. My mother and father were gone. I knew those pieces of granite didn't truly mark their presence. They were somewhere else. But they were not in a place where I could see them, or feel them, or talk to them. And at that moment, I was alone and lonely.

"I turned around and looked at the magnolia tree. It was tall and strong and graceful. And I knew my father would have liked it. All of a sudden, a movement caught my eye and I turned back around, facing the two headstones. And there it was, a bluebird. It had come from who knows where and perched itself on Daddy's headstone. It just stood there, looking at me, cocking its head from side to side. And I just looked at it. A coincidence? A fluke? No. You will never convince me of that. It was a moment I will never forget. After a minute or two the bird flew away, and I was alone again. But the loneliness was gone and the sadness had disappeared. I still miss them, my mother and father. There are times when I miss them more than others. But when I feel their absence the most, I can draw on that moment, on that experience. And I know I'm not really alone."

"Hmm," Paul murmured. "You know, I don't think that was a coincidence either. And that's all I'm looking for. Some kind of sign, something that's real for me, just like that was for you."

"And you will have it, Paul," I told him. "It will come in its own time. Let me tell you one more thing, something that recently happened and that I've only shared with a few people.

"Not too long ago, one of my sons and I were cleaning out the attic. We've lived in our house for more than twenty years and have accumulated a bunch of stuff. Mostly things that should have been thrown out a long time ago. Anyway, I found a big cardboard box way back in one of the corners and was moving it toward the steps, where there was better light. I had no idea what was in it. As I was moving it, the bottom broke and a lot of stuff spilled out. There was a stamp collection I'd had when I was nine or ten years old. And there were my Boy Scout things—merit badges and an old cap. And there was a plastic department-store bag, sealed with some dried-up Scotch tape.

"I picked up the bag and opened it. Inside, I found a bunch of old letters. It was hot up there and I was curious about these letters, so I told my boy I was going downstairs for a minute. If he wanted to take a break, he could go ahead. I went down to our empty guest room and spread the envelopes out on the bed.

"Before I go on, I need to explain a little about what was happening in my life at that time. Or at least in my professional life. My business partner and I were experiencing a difficult situation, one that was requiring a lot of time and thought. And it was becoming very uncomfortable. We were faced with making a decision that could cost us a lot if things didn't go well, but that could eventually put us in a better circumstance. At any rate, we were in a tough spot, and a lot of my mental and emotional energy was consumed with trying to figure out the right thing to do. And sometimes I just wasn't sure.

"Anyway, I looked at these letters and realized they were all addressed to me, and they had been written by my father. The postage dates were during the years I was in medical school, almost thirty years ago. I picked up one of the letters and opened it. It had been a while since I had seen my father's handwriting, and somehow this stunned me. I don't know why it did, but seeing his handwriting…it…it…a lot of things suddenly came back to me. And then it was as if he were right there in the room with me.

"I don't know why I picked up that first letter. I just grabbed one and started reading it. After the first paragraph, I realized why he had written it. I was in my first year of medical school, and during that fall, I was really down. Not that I was having trouble with school. Sure it was tough, but I was doing fine. I was just wondering whether I was in the right place, doing the right thing. I had talked to him about it and told him I was even thinking about doing something different. Looking back on it, and being a father myself as I read that letter, I had a moment of regret for having burdened Daddy with this. But now I realized he had been listening, he had taken me seriously, and he had taken the time to sit down and write this letter to me.

"At that moment, he was right there with me. I could see his face and hear his voice coming to me from the pages I held in my hand. At first, he talked about some of the hard times he had experienced. And then about the difficult situations other family members were going through. Finally, he addressed my situation. And his message to me was clear. I was in the right place and I was doing the right thing. And one thing he said stood out and struck a chord. 'You won't be able to experience the joys of 1974 and 1975 if you don't endure the hardships of 1973.' I remember reading this letter when I was in medical school, and I had known he was right. I had endured that period of my life and had found the other side of that difficult time to be much better and much brighter.

"And suddenly I realized he was talking to me about my present circumstance. He was talking to me right then, thirty years after he wrote those words. He was telling me to endure—to pick the right course and stay with it. To remember that it might exact a cost, but that a better day would come. And I knew then my partner and I were doing the right thing. It was the advice I needed at that moment, the confirmation I had been looking for. And I thanked my father."

I was finished. I wondered if I had said too much to this stranger. But I felt a strange and rare calmness, and was grateful for this moment.

There was no sound from the corner of the room. I got out of the chair, paused briefly by the bed, and turned towards the door.

"Thanks, Dr. Lesslie."

I stopped and looked back at this man, still faceless in the darkened room. "No, I need to thank you, Paul," I told him.

I stepped out into the hallway and closed the door behind me. For a moment I stood there alone, in the quiet. What had begun as an inconvenience had become a gift, a blessing. It was unexpected to be sure, but it was a true blessing.

I walked to the elevator, my father at my side.

15

Who Is My Brother?

*On one occasion an expert in the law stood up to test Jesus.
"Teacher," he asked, "what must I do to inherit eternal life?"*

"What is written in the Law?" he replied. "How do you read it?"

*He answered: "'Love the Lord your God with all your heart
and with all your soul and with all your strength and with all
your mind'; and, 'Love your neighbor as yourself.'" "You have
answered correctly," Jesus replied. "Do this and you will live."*

But Jesus was questioned further: *"Who is my neighbor?"*

In answer he tells the story of the man beaten by robbers and left
for dead, and the response of three different passersby, including the "Good Samaritan." Then he questions his listener:

*"Which of these three do you think was a neighbor to the man
who fell into the hands of robbers?" Jesus asked. The expert
in the law replied, "The one who had mercy on him."*

Jesus told him, "Go and do likewise."

—FROM LUKE 10:25-37

M ost of us are seldom exposed to the reality of the truly destitute,
the truly unfortunate, and the truly untouchable. We see it only
through the aseptic medium of the TV screen or the computer monitor.
In the ER, our exposure is up close and personal. We have to approach
these circumstances from a dispassionate and technical standpoint,
doing the things we are trained to do: stabilize, diagnose, treat. And
then, in a quieter moment, we are left to sort out the more human and
philosophical meaning of what we have just experienced.

Sometimes, we can't even begin to imagine.

∞

"ER, this is Medic 2. Is the doctor nearby?"

I was sitting at the counter of the nurses' station, finishing up the chart of the patient I had just seen in room 3. It was a two-year-old boy with a temp of 104. He had a rip-roaring ear infection but would do fine with antibiotics and something for pain.

Lori picked up the radio receiver and glanced at me, raising her eyebrows in question.

I nodded and glanced at the clock across the hallway. *10:30.* It had been a quiet evening, especially for a Monday. But it was cold outside, low twenties. And though normal for mid-January, cold weather sometimes kept people indoors and at home.

"Medic 2," Lori answered. "Dr. Lesslie is right here. Just a second."

She handed the receiver to me and then walked over to the child in room 3. I placed the receiver in its cradle and punched the speakerphone button.

"This is Dr. Lesslie," I said. "What's going on?"

It wasn't unusual for one of the paramedics to ask to speak to the doctor on duty in the ER. Usually they would be requesting clinical advice for a difficult situation. Sometimes it would be a touchy circumstance, maybe a domestic problem or someone who really didn't need to be transported to the ER by ambulance. I continued to write on the chart, anticipating a straightforward response.

"Doc, Denton Roberts here. We've…" He paused, his voice unsure and troubled.

The puzzling response by the paramedic piqued my interest. I stopped writing and put the chart down.

"Go ahead, Denton. What's going on?"

"It's, uh, a little unusual." He paused again. And then, "We're bringing in a forty-seven-year-old male. Stable, vital signs are okay, but, uh…could you meet us outside, at the ambulance entrance? Our ETA is about five."

Now this *was* an unusual request. The last time I had been asked to meet an ambulance outside the doors of the ER I'd found myself delivering a screaming, full-term little girl. That wasn't going to happen this time, though. There was no panic, no sense of urgency in Denton's voice. Yet something out of the ordinary was going on.

Amy Conners was the unit secretary tonight, and she had been listening to this communication. She pivoted in her chair and looked at me, her lips pursed in puzzlement.

"Uh, sure, Denton. If that's what you need," I responded.

"I would really appreciate it, Doc. We'll be there in four to five. Thanks."

Amy reached over and hit the speaker button on the scanner, ending the call.

"Now what do you think's up with Denton?" she asked me. "He sounded sorta upset."

"He did, didn't he? I guess we'll find out in a minute."

I finished the last notations on the record of our two-year-old, placed the chart in the discharge basket, and walked to the ambulance doors. As I stepped on the activating mat, the doors slowly opened inward. I was buffeted by a blast of cold air, a reminder that it was winter and I was not dressed for lingering very long outdoors.

The lights of the approaching ambulance played over the few cars in the Emergency Department parking area. I glanced up, remarking to myself the clearness of the night sky. I found the new moon, which had just edged past the treeline beyond the parking lot. Just down and to the right…that would be Venus. Bright, stately. And Jupiter would be—

Medic 2 pulled to a stop in front of me, ending my all-too-brief reverie. Glancing through the driver's window, I saw Seth Jones at the wheel. He waved and nodded, then killed the engine. Seth, an EMT, had been Denton's partner for the past five years.

My attention was drawn to the back of the ambulance, where

Denton had opened the double doors from the inside. He stepped down and greeted me as I walked to the rear of the vehicle.

"Thanks for meeting us out here, Doc," he said. "I just thought it would be better if we talked a minute before we bring the patient inside. You might not want us to bring him in at all when you, uh…"

"No problem, Denton," I responded, moving toward the open doors.

He grabbed my arm and I stopped, looking directly in his face.

"Before you step in there, Doc, you need to know something," he told me, his eyes meeting mine.

"What's going on here?" I asked, shivering in the cold night air. I was beginning to lose my patience.

"We got a call to Oak Park from a neighbor of this guy," he began, tilting his head in the direction of the ambulance. "The neighbor said we needed to pick this guy up, that he needed some help. Nothing more specific than that. Then he hung up. So we went over and found this fella in a trailer. No electricity. No heat. Just a kerosene space heater that was out of fuel. Said it had just run out. Maybe he was telling the truth, 'cause the place was cool, but not freezing."

He paused and stamped his feet in the cold air. I shivered again.

"The trailer was in a vacant lot," Denton continued, "surrounded by nothing but trash."

Oak Park was an area well known to EMS and the staff of the ER. It was an unfortunate neighborhood, run down and left behind by a city that was expanding in different and more affluent directions. EMS runs to Oak Park were frequently dangerous, with an inordinate number of gunshots, seizures, and stabbings.

"Says his name is Charlie," Denton informed me. "No last name. No ID. No nothin'. The trailer was a wreck. Just a few empty cans of beans on the floor. Oh, and there were two cats and a mangy dog inside. Didn't even get up when we walked in. Just sorta looked at us." He stopped and rubbed his hands together.

I was trying to decipher the importance of the dog, when Denton continued.

"Charlie's got some kind of skin problem. Had it for a long time, and it's really bothering him now. Itching somethin' fierce, he says. That's the main reason the neighbor called us. That, and the—"

He hadn't finished this last sentence when I broke from his grasp and stepped up into the ambulance. I was cold, and it was time to get me and this patient inside.

The overhead battery-powered lights were on. They were dim, but I could make out the form of our patient lying under a blanket on the ambulance stretcher. The blanket was tucked under his scruffily bearded chin and his large dark eyes were agitated, glancing from side to side. His hair stood in shocks, interspersed with irregular bald areas. The scalp that was visible was a blotched, angry-red color. He was filthy, and had a peculiar odor—a combination of musk, sour clothes, decay, and something else I couldn't quite identify.

My eyes were drawn to his blanketed torso, where I could make out the furious movement of his arms and hands. He was violently scratching himself. And now I could hear his faint moaning. It was a pitiful sight and sound.

"Charlie, I'm Dr. Lesslie," I said to him. "I'm here to help you."

I reached down and grabbed the edge of the blanket. Denton had stepped into the ambulance and was standing behind me. He whispered in my ear.

"I'd be careful with that, Doc," he warned. "Like I said, it's not just the itching that's bothering him…"

I had stopped as Denton said this, but now I lifted the edge of the blanket, pulling it toward me and exposing Charlie's scantily clad body. His dirty and tattered plaid shirt was open, revealing his chest and abdomen. The light was not very good, but I could see that his skin was wrinkled and scaling. That strange odor was stronger now, and I noted oozing from the deep furrows that seemed to be everywhere.

Then I froze and just stared. There was…movement. His skin was moving, writhing, somehow alive. And he was scratching himself everywhere. What was I looking at? I leaned closer. Were those—

"It's the ants, Doc," Denton said. "They're everywhere. All through the trailer, and all over his body. They're itching him to death."

Reflexively I stepped back, dropping the blanket over his body. His eyes caught mine and correctly interpreted my revulsion. Yet his gaze didn't waver.

"Help me," he pleaded.

I collected myself and thought for a minute.

"Denton, ask Seth to take him to room 4. It's empty and he'll have some privacy. Then we'll need to figure this out."

"Sure thing, Doc." He was obviously relieved to be passing the responsibility of this unfortunate man on to someone else. "Seth," he called out. "Come on back here."

Seth rolled Charlie through the ambulance entrance and toward the waiting bed of room 4. I glanced over and watched as Tina Abbott, a young nurse from one of the staffing agencies, followed them into the room. Denton and I stood just inside the automatic doors and he told me what he had learned from the neighbor who had placed the 9-1-1 call.

Charlie had been living in town for about two years. Apparently he moved around a lot, never staying long in any one place. The neighbor owned the lot and the trailer, and one day Charlie had knocked on his door, asking for work and food. He gave him some odd jobs to do and let him mow the grass. The run-down trailer wasn't being used, and he let Charlie stay there for free.

"Not a bad guy," Denton said of the neighbor. "Apparently he took pity on Charlie and would bring him meals every few days. That's how he got to know about him and his problem."

Charlie had been born somewhere in the Midwest, and from about six months of age his parents knew something was wrong. His skin began to wrinkle and then to crack and ooze. At first they were told their child just had a bad case of eczema. They tried various steroid creams, but nothing helped. His skin just got worse. Eventually the correct diagnosis was made. It was a condition called *ichthyosis*. *Ichthy* refers to fish, and their scales were descriptive of this disease. This particular variety spared the face, palms, and soles of the feet. But the rest of the body was affected with varying degrees of scales, cracking, and furrows. There was no cure, and depending upon the severity it could be very difficult to endure. Skin infections were common, as was itching. Interminable itching.

Charlie had a severe case, the worst I had ever seen. When he was two years old, Denton told me his parents had had enough. The constant draining sores, the crying, and the stares and disgust of all who saw him became too much for them to bear. They tried to leave him at several orphanages, but none would accept him. Who would be willing to adopt this child? So finally they just abandoned him. Left him on a park bench and took off.

He had grown up in a series of foster homes, being home-schooled, if it could be called that. No public school would accept him because they thought his skin condition was contagious.

And then he had just wandered from town to town, working where he could find employment. The neighbor didn't know much more than that.

"Just a pitiful creature," he had told the EMTs. "I just finally had to call you guys."

I thanked Denton for the information, and then I noticed a small black ant climbing up his right shirtsleeve. I pointed to it and he brushed it away.

"Aaaah!" The scream came from the direction of room 4. We both looked over in time to see the curtain fly open and Tina Abbott bolt from the room. She had both hands held to her mouth and ran bent over. Running blindly, she stumbled into the soiled-linen cart and knocked it over, spilling its contents.

"Aaaah!" she screamed again, and then began to vomit in the middle of the nurses' station.

Lori had just walked back to the counter from triage, having sent our two-year-old with the ear infection on his way.

"Could you step into room 4?" I asked her. "Seth is in there, and he may need some help."

Without asking any questions, she started in that direction. First she helped Tina sit down on one of the chairs at the desk.

I then turned to Amy Conners. "Would you check the cleaning closet and see if we have any insect spray?"

"What the—" she began.

I just shook my head and said, "Please, just see if we have any, and bring it to room 4."

Lori was attempting to wipe some of the ants off Charlie as I entered the room.

"Hmm," she murmured as I walked over.

The light here was better and now I could see just how severe Charlie's skin condition had become. There were deep crevices everywhere, with no apparent area of healthy skin except on his face, hands, and feet. And the ants were everywhere as well. They were crawling in and out of these cracks and fissures, apparently having made their home there. All the while, Charlie was scratching and quietly moaning.

After ordering something for the itching, I left Lori with Charlie and walked over to the nurses' station. I sat down and began to ponder my options. First, we needed to get these ants off him. But how? Enough insect spray to kill all of these ants would probably be toxic. We couldn't scrub him down—the ants were buried in his skin. Alcohol? Betadine? That wouldn't work.

"What about the Hubbard tank in PT?" This came from Amy, who had sensed my quandary and had come up with the obvious remedy. "You know," she added. "The one over in physical therapy."

This was the perfect solution. This large stainless-steel tank, when filled with warm water, was used to treat patients with burns and other skin injuries. You could suspend a person in the tank and gradually submerge them. In Charlie's case, the ants would either drown or have to flee for survival.

"That's a great idea!" I told her. "Thanks. Could you get the nursing supervisor on the phone and we'll see if we can get this going?"

"That would be May Flanders," she informed me with obvious skepticism in her voice.

"Hmm," I muttered. "Well, get her on the phone, and we'll see."

May Flanders was sixty-two years old and had been a nursing supervisor for about seventy years, it seemed. I had never seen her touch a patient, much less offer any constructive help to our staff, even in the worst of circumstances. Most puzzling was that she always carried a ballpoint pen in one hand and a clipboard in the other. Yet never in all my encounters with her had I ever seen her make any sort of notation on that pad of paper.

Fifteen minutes later, Amy's phone rang.

"ER, this is Amy," she answered, followed by silence as she listened to the caller. "Yeah—well, okay. But why don't you tell him that."

She handed me the phone, shaking her head and silently mouthing, "May Flanders."

I took the receiver. "Ms. Flanders, this is Dr. Lesslie. What did you find out?"

"I talked with Jim Watson, head of PT," May solemnly informed me. "And he said, 'No way.' It will not be possible to use his tank for this purpose. Cleaning it, and…and…you know. Just impossible. So the answer is no. You will just have to find some other means of—"

"There are no other means," I interrupted. My face was flushing, and I was becoming angry. "Why don't you just come down here and look at this guy, and then tell me what we're supposed to do."

There was silence. And then, "I suppose that is your problem, Dr. Lesslie." Then she hung up.

I wanted to throw the phone across the room. But somehow I managed to calm myself and hand it back to Amy.

She hung up the receiver and then looked at me as she tapped the eraser end of her pencil on the desktop.

"What about the administrator on duty? I can find out who that is, if you want," she volunteered.

That was another good idea. It would be going over the head of May Flanders, but that was of no consequence to me at this point. Charlie needed to be taken care of, and we were getting nowhere. And this was just the start. First we had to rid him of the ants, and then we would need to find a physician on staff to admit him to the hospital. That was going to be another significant challenge.

It was 11:45 when Amy again answered the ringing telephone.

"Mr. Waterbury, this is Amy Conners in the ER. Sorry to bother you this late, but Dr. Lesslie needs to speak with you."

Nodding my thanks, I took the receiver. "Ken, Robert Lesslie." Ken Waterbury was one of three assistant administrators. Thirty-five years old, he had made his way through the hospital ranks, having started in the dietary department. I wasn't exactly sure what he did as an assistant, but he had drawn the duty for administrative coverage this night.

I explained Charlie's situation to him and the problems we were having obtaining access to Physical Therapy and the Hubbard tank.

"Well Dr. Lesslie, this is a pickle, isn't it? Have you considered sending him back to his home and notifying social services in the morning? That might be the best solution. After all, you say he has no ID, and I'm sure he has no insurance. We don't want to saddle him with a huge hospital bill, now do we? Perhaps—"

"Ken, this man *has* no home," I explained, feeling my face once again turning red. That's part of my Scottish ancestry, and unfortunately it makes it very difficult for me to disguise my emotions. "If we send him out, he'll die in the cold. And we have to do something about his skin condition. He needs to be admitted to the hospital." I was adamant with this last point.

"Well..." he responded. From the tone of his voice, I knew where this was headed.

"Just a minute, Ken," I said, and then held out the phone at arm's length but where I was sure he would be able to hear what I was saying.

"Ms. Conners, who is the chief of medical staff this year? Isn't it Dr. Burns?"

"Yes, that's right. Dr. Burns," she answered. "And he's on call for his group tonight. Do you want me to get him on the phone?" She had quickly picked up on what I was doing and spoke loud enough for the administrator to hear.

"Yeah, would you? I need to talk with him about this problem."

Ken Waterbury was saying something over the phone, and I again held it to my ear.

"What was that, Ken?" I asked. "I didn't hear you."

"Don't, uh, don't call Dr. Burns just yet. Let me, uh, let me check on a couple of things," he stammered. "I'll get right back to you."

He hung up. I had pushed a button, and knew it. The one thing an assistant administrator didn't want to do was create a big problem, especially in the middle of the night. And Dr. Sandy Burns would do just that. He was the head of the largest orthopedic group in town and had been one of the leading admitters to the hospital for more than twenty years. More important, he was an outspoken champion of patient care and didn't mind butting heads with anyone who stood in the way of achieving that end. Ken Waterbury knew where Sandy Burns would come down on this issue.

As it turned out, I never had to talk with Sandy. Miraculously, somehow, we were able to send Charlie to PT and have him treated in the Hubbard tank. And thankfully this worked. He was soon free of the ants that had plagued him. There was an occasional confused insect that would crawl from a hidden crevice, but it would be quickly removed. He was much more comfortable now, with the ants gone and with the medicine Lori had given him to control his itching.

We managed to find someone to admit him to the hospital for a dermatological evaluation and hopefully some form of treatment. I had no illusion he would be cured—or even substantially improved. But I hoped he could at least be made more comfortable, and that whatever support systems we had in the community for a person like this could be brought into play.

My work schedule didn't bring me back to the ER for three days. When I got the chance, I went upstairs to check on Charlie. He had been admitted to the medical ward on the third floor, room 314. When I got there, the bed was empty. I asked the head nurse of the unit about Charlie. She shook her head and told me he had been discharged two days earlier. She didn't know anything else—not where he went, not about any follow-up. He was just gone.

A few days later, Denton Roberts brought a patient into the ER again, and I had a chance to ask him about Charlie.

"Seen anything more of the guy with the ants?" I asked.

"Nope, Doc. In fact, we were on Oak Park yesterday, and I noticed the trailer was gone. That whole lot is empty. Looks like it was bull-dozed. Don't know what happened to him."

No one did. I never saw Charlie again. And to this day, have heard nothing about him. I sense that he's out there somewhere, alone and miserable.

But we can't fix everybody. Sometimes I wonder if we can really fix anybody. We couldn't fix Charlie. He was one of the invisible people who drift among us, unknown and unloved, one of the "untouch-ables." One of the ones we are called to touch.

I picked up the next chart on the counter. "Sore throat and fever."

What value has compassion that does not take its object in its arms?

ANTOINE DE SAINT EXUPÉRY (1900–1944)

16

Angels in the ER

*Do not forget to entertain strangers, for by so doing some
people have entertained angels without knowing it.*

—Hebrews 13:2

If you don't believe in angels, you should spend some time in the ER.
You will soon learn they do in fact exist, and they manifest themselves in a variety of forms. Some are nurses, a few are doctors, and
many are "everyday people," passing through our doors and into our
lives. Sometimes you have to look hard for their wings. And sometimes
you have to shield your eyes from the glow that surrounds them.

⬥

Macey Love came through the triage door in a wheelchair. She was
leaning forward, tightly gripping the handles of the chair as Lori
pushed her into the department.

"We're going to 5," Lori said. "It's her asthma again."

I was standing on the other side of the counter and had looked up
as they entered. Macey saw me and smiled, nodding her head. She
was struggling for breath, and I could hear her wheezing from across
the room.

"I'll be right there," I told Lori. And then to Amy, "Give Respiratory Therapy a call and tell them Macey is here."

Macey Love was well known to the staff of our emergency department. She was a sixty-two-year-old woman who had suffered with
asthma all of her life. Over the past decade or so the disease had

worsened, necessitating frequent visits to the ER. Usually we could turn one of her asthmatic attacks around with aggressive treatment, keeping her in the department for several hours and watching her closely. She didn't want to be admitted to the hospital and made her feelings perfectly clear on that point. "Dr. Lesslie, I've got to get back home and take care of my two grandchildren, so you'd better get me tuned up," she would tell me, sometimes shaking her index finger for emphasis.

On a few occasions she was too sick to go back home, and we would have to send her upstairs for a few days. Those occasions had become more frequent of late.

Still, we would do everything we could to get her "tuned up" and back home. We knew about her grandchildren and the responsibilities she had with them.

The two girls, eight and ten years old, had been living with their grandmother for the past six years. Their mother had decided to move to New York and had abruptly left them with Macey. She hadn't returned. Sometimes at night or on a weekend, the girls would come to the ER with Macey. We didn't want them sitting in the waiting room alone, so they would come into the ER with their grandmother. They were neat kids, friendly, smiling, and well-behaved.

Macey had devoted this time of her life to caring for these girls. Before asthma had robbed her of her lung capacity, Macey had been the choir director for the largest AME church in town. Each Sunday morning she had made sure her two granddaughters were in the choir loft with her. And on Wednesday night they would be there for choir practice.

Macey was proud of them. It was easy to see that, and they loved her dearly.

The girls weren't with her this day. It was around noon on an April Thursday, and they were in school.

Lori was starting an IV in Macey's left hand as I walked into room 5.

"Pulse ox is 87 percent," she informed me. This number came from a device that was placed over one of her fingertips, pressing gently over the nail bed. It measured the amount of oxygen in Macey's blood, and while 87 was low, I had seen her much worse. "Oxygen going at three liters a minute," Lori added. "Do you want a blood gas?"

Macey winced when she said this, anticipating once again the painful needle stick in her wrist as blood was drawn from the radial artery. It would give us a more complete picture of her oxygenation status, much more so than a simple pulse ox measurement. But it was pretty painful.

"No, let's hold off there and see how she does," I told Lori, to Macey's obvious relief.

Her lungs were really tight today, with audible wheezing but not a lot of air movement. After listening to her chest, I stood back and looked down at her, my arms folded across my chest.

Before I could say anything, she raised her hand and shook a finger at me. She didn't have to say anything, and would have found it difficult to do so between her labored respirations.

"I know, I know, Macey," I said. "We'll do everything we can to keep you out of the hospital. But you're pretty tight this time. You know that."

She nodded, and she was smiling as Lori fitted a mask across her mouth and nose. The mask was connected to a machine that was delivering a vaporized concoction of oxygen, water, and a bronchodilator. Macey knew the routine and was sucking the misty medicine as deeply into her lungs as she could.

We started some other medicine through her IV, and I ordered a portable chest X-ray. We would need to know if a pneumonia or some other problem was contributing to the problem.

I told her what we would be doing and she nodded her head, smiling through the steam that was escaping from the mask on her face.

It was the smile that always struck me. But it was more than just a simple and pleasant smile. There was a twinkle in Macey's eyes, and a glow that seemed to surround her. It didn't matter how sick she was or how bad her asthma was. She was always smiling, and through that smile she was expressing her love. I could clearly see that with her grandchildren. But amazingly, I could see and feel it with us as well, the staff of the ER. I didn't know anyone who was not affected by this, and who didn't want to help take care of Macey when she had to come in for treatment.

Virginia Granger was affected by that smile. But that had been going on for more than fifty years.

Virginia and Macey had both grown up in Rock Hill. When they were in grade school, back in the forties, the schools were segregated. Any "mixing" of the races was frowned upon, if not strictly forbidden. Macey's father had worked at one of the large textile plants in town, as had Virginia's. The two girls had met at one of the company functions, where they had inadvertently bumped into each other. They had become fast friends and had managed to see and play with each other on a regular basis. Macey's disarming spirit and Virginia's tenacity, which brooked no meddling in her personal affairs, withstood the stares and occasional slurs of less enlightened "friends" and townspeople.

This relationship had grown and flourished until time and life choices intervened. Macey finished high school and took a job at a dry-cleaning establishment in town. Virginia had dreamed of becoming a nurse, and she left Rock Hill for college to pursue that career. For years they hadn't seen each other. Only chance had brought them back together. Chance and Macey's asthma.

Several years earlier, Macey had come to the ER in the midst of a severe asthma attack. Virginia and I were working that day, and she was taking care of Macey when I entered her exam room.

"I'm just so glad you are here today, Ginny," Macey had said, looking up at her friend. "I'm glad you'll be the nurse taking care of me."

I had glanced over at Virginia upon hearing this. *Ginny.* Now there was something I could use. Then Virginia looked at me over the top of her glasses, and I knew for certain I would never utter that nickname in her presence.

"You know, Ginny," Macey continued between her gasping respirations, "the Lord has blessed me mightily. He truly has."

She paused to catch her breath and I listened carefully, curious as to how she would continue this thought. She was in the ER, in significant respiratory distress, and suffering from a disease that was not going away. And yet she spoke of being blessed.

I would soon learn about the blessings of Macey Love. She told us about her granddaughters and the many things they did together. She reminded Virginia about her father and the tireless days and nights he had worked to provide for his wife and children. And she told us of her complete lack of fear as she faced the uncertainties of her worsening asthma and failing health. And in the midst of all of that was her smile, and those twinkling eyes.

The only time I had seen that smile even hint at fading was one morning when the two of us were talking about her granddaughters. She was going to have to be admitted to the hospital on this occasion, and she seemed more aware than ever of the gravity of her medical condition.

"Dr. Lesslie," she had said to me. "If something happens to me, I just don't know what will happen to those girls. They're all the world to me, and I'm afraid I'm just about all they have. There's Patrice, my sister, but...I just don't know."

And then she was silent, thinking. She closed her eyes, and after a moment she nodded her head. She opened her eyes, and the smile was back.

On this particular visit, Macey was responding to our treatments. Her breathing was much less labored and her oxygen saturation had improved to 95 percent. We would continue the inhalers and the medications, but I was planning on being able to send her home in an hour or so. She would be relieved, and I walked over to room 5 to let her know.

I pulled the curtain back and Macey looked up at me, smiling. Sitting by the side of her stretcher was Virginia Granger. She glanced up as I entered and then looked back at Macey.

They were holding hands.

I stood there for a moment, watching these two women, these two friends.

"I'll be back in a few minutes," I stammered, and backed out of the room.

Macey is gone now. She died during an asthma attack at home one night before one of our EMS units could reach her. It's been more than fifteen years since I last saw her in the ER, but I can see her face before me now as clearly as if she were in the room with me. I will never forget that smile, those twinkling eyes, and the special feeling we all experienced in her presence.

The writer of the book of Hebrews advises us to always be hospitable, lest we be in the presence of an angel and not realize it. With Macey, I knew.

And with Virginia.

Emma and Sarah Gaithers lived in one of the older neighborhoods in town. The two sisters, both in their eighties now, had lived in the same house all of their lives. Their father had been middle-management in the largest textile mill in the city, and he had built their home when large and square and white was the thing to do.

The family had lived four or five blocks from the mill, comfortably located between the homes of the hourly mill workers and the exclusive neighborhood of the mill owners, the bankers, and the town's doctors.

The textile plant was gone now, and the neighborhood had been left to do the best it could. Many of the houses had been torn down or boarded up, and "For Sale" signs dotted distressed and overgrown yards. The exclusive neighborhoods were now located in the suburbs, but the Gaither sisters remained. In reality, they had nowhere to go. Their parents had died forty years earlier, leaving them with a mortgage-free house and little else.

The fact they had been able to stay in this house was remarkable. Sarah had been a schoolteacher and had taught long enough to qualify for state retirement benefits. But Emma had never been employed. She had suffered some unspecific accident during her delivery and had never developed normally. Her mental age was probably around three or four years, and she had been confined to a wheelchair since the age of five. Her legs were twisted and useless, as was her left arm and hand. She was able to use her right hand, but she had never developed any significant dexterity. After her mother and father died she had been totally dependent on her sister.

Sarah assumed this responsibility unflinchingly. She had attended college and earned her teaching degree, but she had never married. If there had ever been a romantic interest in her life, it was a closely guarded secret. Emma was her only family and had been the focus of her life.

Now in her mid-eighties, Sarah was having a more difficult time taking care of her sister. While Emma did not have any chronic medical problems, Sarah had developed diabetes and hypertension. This was beginning to take its toll. In spite of her dedicated and indomitable spirit, she was growing weaker, and the daily routine of taking care of Emma was becoming more difficult.

"Come on this way, Sarah," I heard Lori say, but I didn't look up.

I was sitting at the foot of bed D in minor trauma, trying to get a suture into the squirming, curling great toe of a noncompliant four-year-old. It was summer, and he had been swimming at the lake and had the misfortune of stepping on a broken bottle. So here he was. For a split second, his toe extended and I grabbed my chance. The curved needle with the suture went through one edge of the laceration and out the other. I cinched the thread firmly, tied it securely in place, and leaned back on the stool.

"There, Momma," I said to the young mother who had ineffectually been trying to control this youngster. "That should do it." She was relieved, as was I.

I looked behind me and diagonally across the room to bed B. Lori was transferring Emma Gaithers from her wheelchair up onto our stretcher. It was an awkward undertaking, helped only by the fact that Emma weighed a little less than 90 pounds. Sarah stood at Emma's side, helping steady her.

Before I could get my gloves off and cross the room to help, Lori had managed to get Emma on the bed and was pulling up the guard-rails. Sarah looked up as I approached.

"Good afternoon, Dr. Lesslie. Good to see you," she said to me. She was holding Emma's alpaca sweater in her hands, gently smoothing the worn garment over her forearm. A sweater, in the middle of July.

"Hello, Sarah," I answered, meeting her eyes and then looking down at her sister. "What's the problem with Emma today?"

The answer seemed obvious. Lori was using sterile gauze to gently clean Emma's forehead. A large laceration extended from her hairline to the bridge of her nose. Blood had clotted in the wound, and the front and collars of her blouse were soaked.

"Hmm," Sarah murmured. "Emma was having her bath, and I was getting her out of the tub. I guess my strength just gave way and she slipped. Her forehead struck the edge of the tub, and...well, you can see what happened," she explained, pointing to her sister's forehead.

Emma was looking up at me while Lori cleaned her face. She was smiling, but it was a vacant smile, and as always I wasn't sure how to respond. I've never known how much she comprehends. Sarah would say that she recognizes us, that she knows the people in the ER. But I've never seen any evidence of that.

Leaning closer to her, I smiled and nodded. "Hello, Emma. Looks like you've got a little cut there." I gently examined the wound, checked her eyes, and looked for any other obvious injuries. Other than the laceration, she looked okay. "We'll get that fixed up in just a minute," I said, patting her shoulder. She continued to smile, but made no sound.

Turning to her sister I said, "She'll need some stitches, probably quite a few. Has she acted like anything else was hurting her?" I asked.

"No, other than that she's fine," Sarah responded. She would know.

To my knowledge, Emma had never uttered a word. Yet she and Sarah communicated in some unspoken way. If Sarah said she was okay, that was enough for me.

"Good," I said. And then I noticed a small but brilliant sparkle of light in the middle of Sarah's left eye.

"Sarah, I thought you were going to get that cataract fixed," I said with feigned sternness. I looked closer and noted that it had gotten larger since she had last been in the ER.

She just shook her head and didn't say anything.

"How's the vision in that eye?" I asked her, taking the ophthalmoscope from its holder on the wall. "Open both eyes real wide," I instructed her while examining her right eye. A cataract was starting in the lens of that eye as well and would soon cloud what remained of her vision.

"Not very good, is it?" I answered for her.

"Dr. Lesslie, how am I supposed to have eye surgery? Who will take care of Emma? I just don't have the time right now. Maybe...maybe in a couple of months or so...We'll just have to wait and see."

"Sarah, it's not going to get better on its own," I gently scolded. "And how are you going to take care of Emma if you can't see?"

We had been down this road before, and we both knew there was no good solution to the dilemma. Sarah and Emma had no other family members, and what few friends they had were either long since dead or were in nursing homes.

One of my younger partners had made a significant mistake on this issue. That mistake had brought the only instance I had ever known Sarah to demonstrate anything resembling anger.

Emma had fallen from bed one night and Sarah had brought her to the ER. After examining her carefully and determining that no serious damage had been done, Jack Young had asked Sarah to step out in the hallway with him. He wanted to speak privately with her about Emma.

"Ms. Gaithers," he began. "Your sister is going to be alright tonight."

"Well that's a relief, Dr. Young," Sarah responded. "I was so worried."

"She's alright *this* time," he went on. "But what about the next time she falls? Or what if something worse happens?" he asked her.

Sarah was startled by the question, and for a moment didn't know how to respond.

Jack Young misinterpreted the pause as an invitation to offer his guidance and wisdom. He proceeded to tell Sarah that it was time for Emma to be placed in a home of some sort. She should be in a place where she would be properly taken care of. In fact, this probably should have happened years ago.

Sarah's face had flushed and her back had stiffened.

"Dr. Young, you don't know me," she had firmly declared. "And you don't know my sister. We have been together for more than eighty years and nothing is going to change that now. I will take care of Emma for as long as the good Lord allows me to."

She paused here and leaned close to his face. "And that, young man, will be His decision and not yours."

She had collected herself, softened, and then said, "If we're finished here, I suppose I should be getting Emma home now. Thank you for your help."

Jack didn't make that mistake again. And while I knew the time for such a move was rapidly approaching, I was not willing to tread there. Not just yet. Sarah would know when her ability to take care of Emma had come to its end.

Several months earlier, I thought we had reached that point. On this occasion Sarah had been the patient and Emma her companion. EMS had brought the two of them to the ER after Sarah had called complaining of cough, fever, and shortness of brief.

We had quickly determined she had a severe pneumonia and would need to be admitted to the hospital for IV antibiotics and supportive care. It would be dangerous to do otherwise.

"Dr. Lesslie, that will be impossible," she had told me, shaking her head. "I cannot stay in the hospital," she stated emphatically. "Who will take care of Emma?"

I again explained the seriousness of her situation, and that should she die, there would be no one to take care of Emma. I got nowhere. She refused to be admitted, and I knew we could not force her.

Exasperated, I left her room and walked over to the nurses' station. Virginia Granger was sitting behind the counter and listened as I voiced my predicament.

She stood up and straightened the starched, pleated skirt of her uniform. "Dr. Lesslie," she said. "Give me a couple of minutes with Sarah."

She walked over to Sarah's room and pulled the curtain closed behind her. I waited. A few minutes later she walked out and around the nurses' station. I caught her eye and was about to speak when her right index finger, pointing upward, silenced me. She went to her office and closed the door behind her.

For fifteen minutes she was on the phone, calling people in administration and on the medical floors. She was calling in every bargaining chip she had, and she had plenty.

When she walked out of her office she was smiling.

"Well, here's the situation," she began telling me. Amy Conners pressed close behind me, curious as to what wonders Virginia had been able to bring about. "The administration has agreed to let Emma stay on a cot in the room with Sarah. The staff on the medical floor will make sure she's fed and taken care of. Sarah should be alright with that, don't you think?"

I didn't know what to say. This kind of thing just didn't happen, not in this hospital.

"Virginia..." I started, and then paused.

"Well, are you going to tell Sarah, or do you want me to?"

Another slight hesitation on my part, and Virginia was on her way to Sarah's room. She agreed to be admitted to the hospital under these terms, and after a week of aggressive therapy, she and Emma were once again at home.

This afternoon's visit to the ER would be more straightforward. We would repair the laceration of Emma's face and the two of them would be on their way.

"Okay, Emma, let's get your forehead taken care of." I spent the next forty-five minutes suturing her laceration. Sarah stood by her side holding her hand, and all the while Emma just stared at the ceiling, smiling. The only indication of any discomfort had been a slight furrowing of her eyebrows as I numbed the edges of the wound.

"There, that should do it," I said, taking off my gloves and tossing them onto the surgical tray.

"Why, Emma," Sarah said, leaning close to her sister, "your forehead looks fine. I think Dr. Lesslie should have been a seamstress."

Emma just smiled. Lori was giving Sarah instructions for wound care as I left the room.

A few minutes later they came up the hall behind me, Sarah pushing the wheelchair and Emma once again in her sweater.

They stopped at the nurses' station and Sarah said, "Thanks again for all your help." She patted her sister's shoulder and added, "And Emma thanks you too."

"You're welcome, Sarah," I answered. "And you too, Emma," I added, looking down at her upturned face. "You two take care of each other."

Sarah nodded and smiled. Then she turned and began pushing the wheelchair again. She paused, confused as to which way she should go. I was about to speak, when Sarah leaned over her sister and said, "Here we go, Emma. This way." They moved across the hall and disappeared through the triage door.

Truly here was a ministering spirit, an angel passing through this life and touching ours.

The ambulance doors opened and Willie James was wheeled into the ER by two thirtysomething women. They were his daughters, and they were pushing his wheelchair toward the nurses' station. One of them looked up at us and said, "It's Daddy's heart again. He's havin' trouble breathin'."

Virginia had just come out of her office carrying the beginnings of next month's nursing schedule. When she saw Willie, she put her stack of papers on the countertop and walked straight over to him.

"Having some trouble tonight, Willie?" she asked, stepping between the two women and taking control of the wheelchair. "Let's just head over this way," she added. She looked at me and nodded in the direction of the Cardiac room.

Willie James was 63 years old. He had suffered a pretty significant heart attack three years ago, leaving him with a little less than half of his cardiac muscle. Since then he had teetered on the edge of heart failure, sometimes doing well, and sometimes slipping over into dangerous and deadly territory. Too much salt, too much stress, too much physical activity—any of a number of things would overload his heart, and fluid would back into his lungs. He would become more and more short of breath, unable to walk short distances or even lie down without gasping for air. Then a frothy foam would form on his lips. Patients sometimes describe this as a feeling of "drowning in your own secretions," and it is understandably very frightening.

Tonight Willie had slipped over the edge, but he was calm, and he even managed to smile up at Virginia as she had walked over to him. He was too short of breath to answer her question and only nodded his head as he leaned forward in the wheelchair, tightly grasping the handles and gasping for breath. The telltale foam of congestive heart failure was evident on his lips.

Willie was wearing an old T-shirt and well-worn plaid trousers. His feet were covered with white athletic socks, one of which had fallen halfway off. Its tattered and dirty toe was dragging on the floor. I got up from behind the counter and followed him and Virginia into the Cardiac room.

Without being asked, Amy said, "I'll get X-ray down here. And the lab and someone from Respiratory."

"Thanks," I responded, glancing at the clock on the wall. *10:35 p.m.*

Willie was in bad shape. He had waited a little too long this time before asking for help. He wasn't responding to our usual treatments, and his condition was deteriorating right before us. And he was getting tired. Virginia was setting up an airway tray, anticipating we would soon have to intubate him and put him on a ventilator. That would be the next step, but I wanted to avoid it if at all possible. Willie did as well. He glanced at the tray with its various equipment and tubes, and his eyes widened. He looked up at me. He couldn't say anything, but his eyes spoke for him.

We were all thankful when he began to improve. His oxygen saturation began to move upward and his pulse slowed a little. We continued our treatments, and within forty-five minutes it was evident he was moving in the right direction. He would avoid the ventilator tonight but would obviously need to be admitted to the hospital.

"Willie, isn't Angus Gaines your doctor?" I asked, making sure that only a movement of his head was required for a response. I was pretty certain that was correct.

He nodded in affirmation.

"Good. I'll give him a call and tell him you're here," I went on. "You'll need to come into the hospital tonight, alright?"

It wasn't a question, and Willie again nodded his head.

A few minutes later, Amy had Dr. Gaines on the phone.

Angus Gaines was in his early seventies and was still practicing medicine full-time. He had been in Rock Hill for more than forty years, and while technically a GP (general practitioner), he took care of just about everything. He didn't do any surgery now, but he had more patients than any other physician in the area, and he wanted to be involved in their care. I knew he would want to know Willie was in the ER. He would probably come in and see him, and then have one of the cardiologists on staff admit him to the CCU.

Angus always came in to see his patients. It didn't matter what time of day or day of the week it might be. We'd give him a call, and within a matter of minutes he would come walking into the department. That wasn't necessarily the rule for other members of the medical staff. In fact, it was becoming the exception.

Only a few days earlier, a forty-year-old woman had come to the ER complaining of fever, chills, and chest pain. She had a history of worsening lupus—an inflammatory disease of the internal connective tissues—and had recently been diagnosed with kidney failure. We determined she had pericarditis complicating her lupus. This was an infection of the outer lining of her heart, and could prove fatal. She would need to be admitted to the hospital. She gave me the name of her family physician and I asked Amy get him on the phone.

A few minutes later she handed me the receiver and I talked with her doctor.

After explaining the circumstances of this patient, I was told, "Well, Robert, we do see this lady in the office, but she owes us money now, and…well…I just don't think we're going to take care of her anymore. Why don't you have the person on call for 'unassigned medicine' admit her."

I was incensed. His response was totally inappropriate. But I knew this was not the time to fight this battle.

I glanced over at our patient, glad she had not been able to hear this conversation. Trying to control my anger and my tongue, I looked at the on-call board, which was located on a column in the nurses' station. It listed the physicians responsible for various specialties: surgery, ortho, pediatrics, medicine. These medical staff members were required to take care of patients who didn't have a doctor.

Locating the "medicine" slot, I read—

"Yeah, Robert—just have the on-call doc—" he began, repeating himself.

"Well, just a minute, Jake," I interrupted him, with not a small feeling of satisfaction and sense of divine justice. "That would be you. You're on call tonight for unassigned medicine."

"Wha…"

We would never get such a response from Angus Gaines. In fact, I had never heard him utter a cross word or show any sign of frustration with his patients or with being called in to the hospital late at night.

This night was no different. I was standing in front of the counter, when Amy handed the phone to me. "It's Dr. Gaines," she told me.

"Angus, this is Robert Lesslie in the ER," I said, wondering if we had waked him. "I've got one of your patients here, Willie James. He's in congestive heart failure again, and he needs to come in."

While I waited for the response, I slid Willie's chart over so I could read the information at the top of it. I knew what was coming, and I wanted to be ready.

"Willie James, you say." The gravelly voice sounded in my ear. Angus seemed wide awake, so maybe we hadn't disturbed his sleep. "Does he live at 122 Bird Street?"

I looked for the address on the chart. "Yep, that's right," I answered. As always, I was amazed by his memory. He knew where just about every one of his patients lived, and there were a lot of them.

"And he was born, uh, sometime in April of 1930," he added.

I looked at the chart again. "Birth date: 4/18/30." How did he do that?

"Yes, you're right again," I told him.

"Okay, yeah, I know Willie. I'll be over directly."

I handed the phone back to Amy, knowing what "directly" meant. He would be here within fifteen minutes.

But how did he do that? How does someone have that kind of memory? I have trouble remembering my wife's anniversary date, and that should be easy, since it's the same as mine.

Still, for Angus Gaines at his age to possess such a memory was an impressive thing. It occurred to me that a large part of his motivation for remembering these things was the genuine care he had for his people.

The ambulance doors were hissing open, and I looked up at the clock. *12:22 a.m.* It had been eleven minutes since I had hung up the phone, and here was Angus coming through the doors.

"Good evening, Robert," he said. "Where is Willie tonight?"

I motioned toward the Cardiac room and stepped in that direction.

Anyone not knowing Dr. Angus Gaines would probably have been startled by his appearance. Amy and I were accustomed to it and we barely noticed.

Angus walked toward Cardiac. He was wearing a knee-length charcoal overcoat, and under the coat the legs of his pin-striped pajamas were clearly visible. On his feet he wore brown leather bedroom slippers. He took off his gray derby hat and tossed it on the countertop.

"So you think he's doing a little better?" he asked me.

I was giving him a brief update as he pushed open the door and we stepped into the room. Willie's daughters were now with him, and one stood on each side of his stretcher. All three looked in our direction as we entered.

You would have thought it was Christmas morning. When they saw Angus Gaines, their eyes lit up and smiles spread across their faces. One of the daughters ran across the room and hugged him. "We're so glad you're here!" she said.

Thirty minutes later they were all on their way to the CCU. Angus picked up his hat at the nurses' station and turned to me. "Thanks for looking after Willie. I'm just going upstairs to make sure he gets settled in. I'll have one of the cardiologists come and take a look at him too."

Then everyone was around the corner and gone, with Angus padding down the hall in his slippered feet.

The rest of my shift was uneventful, with only a few patients scattered during the early morning hours. My relief walked into the department at five till seven, and I grabbed my briefcase and headed out the ambulance doors.

The early morning air was clean and cool, and the sun was trying to peek over the trees at the far end of the doctors' parking lot. I walked up the hill toward my car and for the first time realized how tired and sleepy I was. I looked forward to getting home, taking a shower, and going to bed.

My attention was drawn by some movement behind and to the left of me. I stopped and turned around. Someone was walking across the far side of the parking lot. I could make out the figure of a man dressed in a dark overcoat and derby hat. It was Angus Gaines. He was just now leaving the hospital, having spent the entire night in Willie James's room, unwilling to leave his side until he knew everything was stable and Willie was going to be all right.

His hands were thrust deep into his pockets, and he shuffled along in his bedroom slippers, obviously deep in thought. For a moment I looked on in admiration as he slowly made his way up the hill. And then something strange and amazing happened as I stood and watched. A single beam of early morning light made its way through the trees, and it shone directly on this remarkable man.

> *We are like children, who stand in the need of masters to*
> *enlighten us and direct us; God has provided for this, by*
> *appointing His angels to be our teachers and guides.*
> —Thomas Aquinas

Notes

Page 47: "Every man naturally desires…" Thomas à Kempis, *The Imitation of Christ* (Peabody, MA: Hendrickson Publishers, 2005), p. 4.

Page 194: "You have to have a lot…" Stanislaw Lec, *Unkempt Thoughts* (New York: St. Martin's Press, 1962) p. 110.

Page 218: "What value has compassion…" Antoine de Saint Exupéry, *The Wisdom of the Sands* (New York: Harcourt Brace and Company, 1950), p. 26.

Page 236: "We are like children…" Thomas Aquinas, *Summa Theologica* (Denton, TX: Christian Classics, reprint ed. 1981).

Other Books You'll Enjoy from Harvest House Publishers

FOUR PAWS FROM HEAVEN
Devotions for Dog Lovers
M.R. Wells, Kris Young, and Connie Fleishauer

Friend, family member, guardian, comforter—a dog can add so much to our lives. These furry, four-footed creatures truly are wonderful gifts from a loving Creator to bring joy, laughter, and warmth to our hearts and homes. These delightful devotions will make you smile and perhaps grow a little misty as you enjoy true stories of how God watches over and provides for us even as we care for our canine companions.

PURR-ABLES FROM HEAVEN
Devotions for Cat Lovers
M.R. Wells, Connie Fleishauer, and Dottie Adams

For those with the right cat-itude, there is nothing like a nice kitty to make life great. Cat people love cats not because they are purr-fect, but in spite of their flaws. These entertaining and enlightening devotions will delight you as you discover how God daily draws us to Himself, provides for our every need, and loves us purr-fectly in spite of our flaws.

THE WHISPERS OF ANGELS
Stories to Touch Your Heart
Annette Smith

This touching collection of true stories will help you find a heavenly perspective in the midst of everyday experiences...as you meet people like Hope, a ten-year-old blind girl who found her place in a brand-new school; or Sam and Lily, childhood sweethearts whose love never stopped growing; or Mr. Simmons, a heart-attack patient who taught his nurse about proper healing. Take a few moments to stop and listen, and perhaps you too will hear the sounds of heaven—*The Whispers of Angels.*

LET'S PLAY BALL
Legends and Lessons from America's Favorite Pastime
Stories by Al Janssen, with paintings by Jim Daly

"Take Me Out to the Ball Game…"

> *The magic of a summer evening at the stadium…*
> *The sound of a fastball smacking into the catcher's mitt…*
> *The aroma of mustard on a warm hot dog…*
> *Friends and families making memories together…*

These little slices of life in the ballpark will remind you why we love this game so much—and will offer you lessons for life from America's favorite pastime.

THE LEGEND OF THE FIREFISH
An Epic Saga of the Pursuit of Faith and Honor
George Bryan Polivka

Packer Throme longs to bring prosperity back to his fishing village by discovering the trade secrets of Scat Wilkins, a notorious pirate who now seeks to hunt the legendary Firefish and sell its rare meat.

Packer begins his quest by stowing away aboard Scat's ship, the Trophy Chase, bound for the open sea. Though he is armed with the love of a priest's daughter, Panna Seline, and a hard-won mastery of the sword, many tests of his courage and resolve follow—beginning when he is discovered by Scat Wilkins himself.

Packer and Panna's epic struggle of faith makes *The Legend of the Firefish* a compelling story that will be enjoyed worldwide by fans of adventure, fantasy, and visionary tales of honor, conflict, and sacrifice.

Book One of the Trophy Chase Trilogy by author George Bryan Polivka

HARVEST HOUSE PUBLISHERS